Card 3

IN QUEST OF THE PERFECT BOOK

A book is a portion of the eternal mind
caught in its progress through the world
stamped in an instant, and preserved for
eternity. — *Lord Houghton* (1809-1885)

IN QUEST OF THE PERFECT BOOK

REMINISCENCES
& REFLECTIONS
OF A BOOKMAN

WILLIAM DANA ORCUTT

PUBLISHED · MCMXXVI · BOSTON
LITTLE, BROWN & COMPANY

THE AUTHOR is indebted to the *Atlantic Monthly* for permission to reprint as the first chapter of this volume an essay which originally appeared in that magazine; to the *Christian Science Monitor* for permission to use, in quite different form, certain material which has been drawn upon in literary editorials written by him for its columns; to Alban Dobson, *Esq.*, G. Bernard Shaw, *Esq.*, Henry James, *Esq.*, Mrs. Anne Cobden-Sanderson, and others, for permission to print personal letters and photographs.

To ITALY
That great Country whose Master-Spirits
in Art, Typography, and Literature
have contributed most toward
THE PERFECT BOOK
this Volume is Dedicated

CONTENTS

CONTENTS

ILLUSTRATIONS

ILLUSTRATIONS

ILLUSTRATIONS

ILLUSTRATIONS

ILLUSTRATIONS

CHAPTER I
In Quest of the Perfect Book

I

IN QUEST OF THE PERFECT BOOK

"HERE is a fine volume," a friend remarked, handing me a copy of *The Ideal Book,* written and printed by Cobden-Sanderson at the Doves Press.

"It is," I assented readily, turning the leaves, and enjoying the composite beauty of the careful typography, and the perfect impression upon the soft, handmade paper with the satisfaction one always feels when face to face with a work of art. "Have you read it?"

"Why—no," he answered. "I picked it up in London, and they told me it was a rare volume. You don't necessarily read rare books, do you?"

My friend is a cultivated man, and his attitude toward his latest acquisition irritated me; yet after thirty years of similar disappointments I should not have been surprised. How few, even among those interested in books, recognize the fine, artistic touches that constitute the difference between the commonplace and the distinguished! The volume under discussion was written by an authority foremost in the art of bookmaking; its producer was one of the few great master-printers and binders in the history of the world; yet the only significance it possessed to its owner was the fact that some one in whom he had confidence had told him it was rare! Being rare, he coveted the treasure, and acquired it with no greater understanding than if it had been a piece of Chinese jade.

"What makes you think this is a fine book?" I inquired, deliberately changing the approach.

He laughed consciously. "It cost me nine guineas—and I like the looks of it."

Restraint was required not to say something that might have affected our friendship unpleasantly, and friendship is a precious thing.

"Do something for me," I asked quietly. "That is a short book. Read it through, even though it is rare, and then let us continue this conversation we have just begun."

A few days later he invited me to dine with him at his club. "I asked you here," he said, "because I don't want any one, even my family, to hear what I am going to admit to you. I have read that book, and I'd rather not know what you thought of my consummate ignorance of what really enters into the building of a well-made volume—the choice of type, the use of decoration, the arrangement of margins. Why, bookmaking is an art! Perhaps I should have known that, but I never stopped to think about it."

One does have to stop and think about a well-made book in order to comprehend the difference between printing that is merely printing and that which is based upon art in its broadest sense and upon centuries of precedent. It does require more than a gleam of intelligence to grasp the idea that the basis of every volume ought to be the thought expressed by the writer; that the type, the illustrations, the decorations, the paper, the binding, simply combine to form the vehicle to convey that expression to the reader. When, however, this fact is once absorbed, one cannot fail to understand that if these various parts, which compositely comprise the whole, fail to harmonize with the subject and with each other, then the vehicle does not perform its full and proper function.

I wondered afterward if I had not been a bit too superior in my attitude toward my friend. As a matter of fact, printing as an art has returned to its own only within the last quarter-century. Looking back to 1891, when I began to serve my apprenticeship under John Wilson at the old University Press in Cambridge, Massachusetts, the broadness of the profession that I was adopting as

my life's work had not as yet unfolded its unlimited possibilities. At that time the three great
American printers were John Wilson, Theodore
L. De Vinne, and Henry O. Houghton. The
volumes produced under their supervision were
perfect examples of the best bookmaking of the
period, yet no one of these three men looked upon
printing as an art. It was William Morris who
in modern times first joined these two words
together by the publication of his magnificent
Kelmscott volumes. Such type, such decorations,
such presswork, such sheer, composite beauty!

This was in 1895. Morris, in one leap, became
the most famous printer in the world. Every one
tried to produce similar volumes, and the resulting
productions, made without appreciating the significance of decoration combined with type, were
about as bad as they could be. I doubt if, at the
present moment, there exists a single one of these
sham Kelmscotts made in America that the printer
or the publisher cares to have recalled to him.

When the first flair of Morris' popularity passed
away, and his volumes were judged on the basis
of real bookmaking, they were classified as marvelously beautiful *objets d'art* rather than books—
composites of Burne-Jones, the designer, and William Morris, the decorator-printer, co-workers in

GUTENBERG

JOHN GUTENBERG, *c.* 1400-1468
From Engraving by Alphonse Descaves
Bibliothèque Nationale, Paris

sister arts; but from the very beginning Morris' innovations showed the world that printing still belonged among the fine arts. The Kelmscott books awoke in me an overwhelming desire to put myself into the volumes I produced. I realized that no man can give of himself beyond what he possesses, and that to make my ambition worth accomplishing I must absorb and make a part of myself the beauty of the ancient manuscripts and the early printed books. This led me to take up an exhaustive study of the history of printing.

Until then Gutenberg's name, in my mind, had been preëminent. As I proceeded, however, I came to know that he was not really the "inventor" of printing, as I had always thought him to be; that he was the one who first foresaw the wonderful power of movable types as a material expression of the thought of man, rather than the creator of anything previously unknown. I discovered that the Greeks and the Romans had printed from stamps centuries earlier, and that the Chinese and the Koreans had cut individual characters in metal.

I well remember the thrill I experienced when I first realized—and at the time thought my discovery was original!—that, had the Chinese or the Saracens possessed Gutenberg's wit to join these letters

7

together into words, the art of printing must have found its way to Constantinople, which would have thus become the center of culture and learn- ing in the fifteenth century.

From this point on, my quest seemed a part of an Arabian Nights' tale. Cautiously opening a door, I would find myself in a room containing treasures of absorbing interest. From this room there were doors leading in different directions into other rooms even more richly filled; and thus onward, with seemingly no end, to the fascinating rewards that came through effort and perseverance.

Germany, although it had produced Guten- berg, was not sufficiently developed as a nation to make his work complete. The open door led me away from Germany into Italy, where literary zeal was at its height. The life and customs of the Italian people of the fifteenth century were spread out before me. In my imagination I could see the velvet-gowned agents of the wealthy patrons of the arts searching out old manuscripts and giving commissions to the scribes to prepare hand-lettered copies for their masters' libraries. I could mingle with the masses and discover how eager they were to learn the truth in the matter of religion, and the cause and the remedies of moral and material evils

8

by which they felt themselves oppressed. I could share with them their expectant enthusiasm and confidence that the advent of the printing press would afford opportunity to study description and argument where previously they had merely gazed at pictorial design. I could sense the desire of the people for books, not to place in cabinets, but to read in order to know; and I could understand why workmen who had served apprenticeships in Germany so quickly sought out Italy, the country where princes would naturally become patrons of the new art, where manuscripts were ready for copy, and where a public existed eager to purchase their products.

While striving to sense the significance of the conflicting elements I felt around me, I found much of interest in watching the scribes fulfilling their commissions to prepare copies of original manuscripts, becoming familiar for the first time with the primitive methods of book manufacture and distribution. A monastery possessed an original manuscript of value. In its *scriptorium* (the writing office) one might find perhaps twenty or thirty monks seated at desks, each with a sheet of parchment spread out before him, upon which he inscribed the words that came to him in the droning, singsong voice of the reader selected for

9

the duty because of his familiarity with the subject matter of the volume. The number of desks the *scriptorium* could accommodate determined the size of this early "edition."

When these copies were completed, exchanges were made with other monasteries that possessed other original manuscripts, of which copies had been made in a similar manner. I was even more interested in the work of the secular scribes, usually executed at their homes, for it was to these men that the commissions were given for the beautiful humanistic volumes. As they had taken up the art of hand lettering from choice or natural aptitude instead of as a part of monastic routine, they were greater artists and produced volumes of surpassing beauty. A still greater interest in studying this art of hand lettering lay in the knowledge that it soon must become a lost art, for no one could doubt that the printing press had come to stay.

Then, turning to the office of Aldus, I pause for a moment to read the legend placed conspicuously over the door:

Whoever thou art, thou art earnestly requested by Aldus to state thy business briefly and to take thy departure promptly. In this way thou mayest be of service even as

ALDUS MANUTIUS, 1450-1515
From Engraving at the British Museum

was Hercules to the weary Atlas, for this is a place of work for all who may enter

But inside the printing office I find Aldus and his associates talking of other things than the books in process of manufacture. They are discussing the sudden change of attitude on the part of the wealthy patrons of the arts who, after welcoming the invention of printing, soon became alarmed by the enthusiasm of the people, and promptly reversed their position. No wonder that Aldus should be concerned as to the outcome! The patrons of the arts represented the culture and wealth and political power of Italy, and they now discovered in the new invention an actual menace. To them the magnificent illuminated volumes of the fifteenth century were not merely examples of decoration, but they represented the tribute that this cultured class paid to the thought conveyed, through the medium of the written page, from the author to the world. This jewel of thought they considered more valuable than any costly gem. They perpetuated it by having it written out on parchment by the most accomplished scribes; they enriched it by illuminated embellishments executed by the most famous artists; they protected it with bindings in which they actually inlaid gold and silver and jewels. To have this thought cheapened by reproduction through the commonplace medium of mechanical printing wounded their æsthetic sense. It was an expression of real love of the book that prompted Bisticci, the agent of so powerful a patron as the Duke of Urbino, to write of the Duke's splendid collection in the latter part of the fifteenth century:

In that library the books are all beautiful in a superlative degree, and all written by the pen. There is not a single one of them printed, for it would have been a shame to have one of that sort.

Aldus is not alarmed by the solicitude of the patrons for the beauty of the book. He has always known that in order to exist at all the printed book must compete with the written volume; and he has demonstrated that, by supplying to the accomplished illuminators sheets carefully printed on parchment, he can produce volumes of exquisite beauty, of which no collector need be ashamed. Aldus knows that there are other reasons behind the change of front on the part of the patrons. Libraries made up of priceless manuscript volumes are symbols of wealth, and through wealth comes power. With the multiplication of printed books this prestige will be lessened, as the masses will be enabled to possess the same gems of thought in less extravagant and expensive form. If, moreover, the people are enabled to read, criticism, the sole property of the scholars, will come into their hands, and when they once learn self-reliance from their new intellectual development they are certain to attack dogma and political oppression, even at the risk of martyrdom. The princes and patrons of Italy are intelligent enough to know that their self-centered political power is doomed if the new art of printing secures a firm foothold.

What a relief to such a man as Aldus when it became fully demonstrated that the desire on the part of the people to secure books in order to learn was too great to be overcome by official mandate or insidious propaganda! With what silent satis-faction did he settle back to continue his splendid work! The patrons, in order to show what a poor thing the printed book really was, gave orders to the scribes and the illuminators to prepare volumes for them in such quantities that the art of hand lettering received a powerful impetus, as a result of which the hand letters themselves attained their highest point of perfection. This final struggle on the part of the wealthy overlords resulted only in redoubling the efforts of the artist master-printers to match the beauty of the written volumes with the products from their presses.

These Arabian Nights' experiences occupied me from 1895, when Morris demonstrated the unlimited possibilities of printing as an art, until 1901, when I first visited Italy and gave myself an opportunity to become personally acquainted with the historical landmarks of printing, which previously I had known only from study. In Florence it was my great good fortune to become intimately acquainted with the late Doctor Guido Biagi, at that time librarian of the Laurenziana and the Riccardi libraries, and the custodian of the Medici, the Michelangelo, and the da Vinci archives. I like to think of him as I first saw him then, sitting on a bench in front of one of the carved *plutei* designed by Michelangelo, in the wonderful *Sala di Michelangiolo* in the Laurenziana Library, studying a beautifully illuminated volume resting before him, which was fastened to the desk by one of the famous old chains. He greeted me with an old-school courtesy. When he discovered my genuine interest in the books he loved, and realized that I came as a student eager to listen to the master's word, his face lighted up and we were at once friends.

In the quarter of a century which passed from this meeting until his death we were fellow students, and during that period I never succeeded in exhausting the vast store of knowledge he possessed,

14

Dott. Comm. GUIDO BIAGI
Seated at one of the *plutei* in the
Laurenziana Library, Florence (1906)

even though he gave of it with the freeſt generosity. From him I learned for the firſt time of the far-reaching influence of the humaniſtic movement upon everything that had to do with the *litteræ humaniores,* and this new knowledge enabled me to cryſtallize much that previously had been fugi-tive. "The humaniſt," Doctor Biagi explained to me, "whether ancient or modern, is one who holds himself open to receive Truth, unprejudiced as to its source, and—what is more important—after having received Truth realizes his obligation to the world to give it out again, made richer by his personal interpretation."

This humaniſtic movement was the forerunner and the essence of the Renaissance, being in reality a revolt againſt the barrenness of mediævalism. Until then ignorance, superſtition, and tradition had confined intellectual life on all sides, but the little band of humaniſts, headed by Petrarch, put forth a claim for the mental freedom of man and for the full development of his being. As a part of this claim they demanded the recognition of the rich humanities of Greece and Rome, which were proscribed by the Church. If this claim had been poſtponed another fifty years, the actual man-uscripts of many of the present standard classics would have been loſt to the world.

The significance of the humanistic movement in its bearing upon the Quest of the Perfect Book is that the invention of printing fitted exactly into the Petrarchian scheme by making it possible for the people to secure volumes that previously, in their manuscript form, could be owned only by the wealthy patrons. This was the point at which Doctor Biagi's revelation and my previous study met. The Laurenziana Library contains more copies of the so-called humanistic manuscripts, produced in response to the final efforts on the part of patrons to thwart the increasing popularity of the new art of printing, than any other single library. Doctor Biagi proudly showed me some of these treasures, notably Antonio Sinibaldi's *Virgil*. The contrast between the hand lettering in these volumes and the best I had ever seen before was startling. Here was a hand letter, developed under the most romantic and dramatic conditions, which represented the apotheosis of the art. The thought flashed through my mind that all the types in existence up to this point had been based upon previous hand lettering less beautiful and not so perfect in execution.

"Why is it," I demanded excitedly, "that no type has ever been designed based upon this hand lettering at its highest point of perfection?"

HAND-WRITTEN HUMANISTIC CHARACTERS
From Sinibaldi's *Virgil*, 1485
Laurenziana Library, Florence [12 x 8 inches]

Doctor Biagi looked at me and shrugged his shoulders. "This, my friend," he answered, smiling, "is your opportunity."

At this point began one of the most fascinating and absorbing adventures in which any one interested in books could possibly engage. At some time, I suppose, in the life of every typographer comes the ambition to design a special type, so it was natural that the idea contained in Doctor Biagi's remark should suggest possibilities which filled me with enthusiasm. I was familiar with the history of the best special faces, and had learned how difficult each ambitious designer had found the task of translating drawings into so rigid a medium as metal; so I reverted soberly and with deep respect to the subject of type design from the beginning.

In studying the early fonts of type, I found them exact counterfeits of the best existing forms of hand lettering at that time employed by the scribes. The first italic font cut by Aldus, for instance, is said to be based upon the thin, inclined handwriting of Petrarch. The contrast between these slavish copies of hand-lettered models and the mechanical precision of characters turned out by modern type founders made a deep impression. Of the two I preferred the freedom of the earliest types, but appreciated how ill adapted these models were to the requirements of typography. A hand-lettered page, even with the inevitable irregularities, is pleasing because the scribe makes a slight variation in forming the various characters. When, however, an imperfect letter is cut in metal, and repeated many times upon the same page, the irregularity forces itself unpleasantly upon the eye. Nicolas Jenson was the first to realize this, and in his famous Roman type he made an exact interpretation of what the scribe intended to accomplish in each of the letters, instead of copying any single hand letter, or making a composite of many hand designs of the same character. For this reason the Jenson type has not only served as the basis of the best standard Roman fonts down to the present time, but has also proved the inspiration for later designs of distinctive type faces, such as William Morris' Golden type, and Emery Walker's Doves type.

William Morris' experience is an excellent illustration of the difficulties a designer experiences. He has left a record of how he studied the Jenson type with great care, enlarging it by photography, and redrawing it over and over again before he began designing his own letter. When he actually produced his Golden type the design was far too much inclined to the Gothic to resemble the model he

64 Quivi il lasciammo, che più non ne narro;
ma negli orecchi mi percosse un duolo,
per ch'io avanti intento l'occhio sbarro.

67 Lo buon maestro disse: "Omai, figliuolo,
s'appressa la città c'ha nome Dite,
coi gravi cittadin, col grande stuolo."

70 E io: "Maestro, già le sue meschite
là entro certo nella valle cerno
vermiglie, come se di foco uscite

73 fossero". Ed ei mi disse: "Il foco eterno
ch'entro le affoca, le dimostra rosse,
come tu vedi in questo basso Inferno."

64. "che": sicchè. Dopo aver narrato come l'ira ha il suo inferno in sè stessa, non rimaneva qui a Dante altro da dire. * vv. 65-81 " La città che ha nome Dite". Dante ode grida di dolore e spalanca gli occhi guardando avanti. "È Dite" osserva il duce. "Veggo già" risponde Dante "le sue meschite, rosse come ferro rovente". "Ciò deriva" spiega Virgilio "dal fuoco eterno che arde là dentro". Giunti ai valli della città infernale, Flegiàs addita l'entrata, e intima ai Poeti di sbarcare. – 65. "duolo": doloroso lamento, che veniva da Dite, e propriamente dai "gravi cittadini" dal "grande stuolo" di cui Virgilio fa subito parola, vedendo Dante guardare in avanti con l'occhio sbarrato per capire donde e da chi venga esso "duolo". – 66. "sbarro": spalanco.

– 68. "Dite": la parte inferiore dell'Inferno, che prende il nome da Dite (latino "Dis"), o Lucifero, "l'imperador del doloroso regno"; confronta Inferno XI, 65; XII, 39; XXXIV, 20. – 69. "gravi": di colpa e di pena; "stuolo": moltitudine. "Est enim ista civitas populosa e plena gentibus totius mundi quae habitant in diversis vicis"; Benvenuti. – 70. "meschite": moschee (confronta Parodi, "Bull." III, 153); così chiamansi le chiese dei Mussulmani; e simili ad esse pare che Dante si figurasse le fortezze della città infernale. Forse vuol dire con ciò, che la religione di Maometto trae sua origine dall'Inferno. "La barca si è già tanto accostata all'altra riva di Stige, che Dante comincia a vedere nelle fossate esterne della città le sue torri infocate, ch'ei chiama "meschite", forse per alludere ai miscredenti che là sono; poichè con un tal nome i Saraceni chiamano i templi del falso lor culto"; Rossetti. – 71. "certo": chiaramente; "cerno" latinismo, vedo. Chiama "valle" il sesto cerchio, il quale sembra giacere sopra lo stesso ripiano del quinto, ma ne è separato da fosse, mura e "meschite", ed offre l'aspetto di città fortificata. – 72. "vermiglie": rosse infocate, come le arche là dentro. – 75. "basso": in cui si puniscono i peccati di malizia e di bestialità, mentre nell'alto Inferno, fuori di Dite, sono puniti i peccati d'incontinenza; confronta Inferno XI, 70-90. – 76. "pur":

Specimen Page of proposed Edition of Dante. To be
printed by Bertieri, of Milan, in Humanistic Type [8¼ x 6

selected. His Troy and Chaucer types that followed showed the strong effect of the German influence that the types of Schoeffer, Mentelin, and Gunther Zainer made upon him. The Doves type is based flatly upon the Jenson model; yet it is an absolutely original face, retaining all the charm of the model, to which is added the artistic genius of the designer. Each receives its personality from the understanding and interpretation of the creator (*pages* 22, 23).

From this I came to realize that it is no more necessary for a type designer to express his individuality by adding or subtracting from his model than for a portrait painter to change the features of his subject because some other artist has previously painted it. Wordsworth once said that the true portrait of a man shows him, not as he looks at any one moment of his life, but as he really looks all the time. This is equally true of a hand letter, and explains the vast differences in the cut of the same type face by various foundries and for the type-setting machines. All this convinced me that, if I were to make the humanistic letters the model for my new type, I must follow the example of Emery Walker rather than that of William Morris.

During the days spent in the small, cell-like alcove which had been turned over for my use in the Laurenziana Library, I came so wholly under the influence of the peculiar atmosphere of antiquity that I felt myself under an obsession of which I have not been conscious before or since. My enthusiasm was abnormal, my efforts tireless. The world out-side seemed very far away, the past seemed very near, and I was indifferent to everything except the task before me. This curious experience was perhaps an explanation of how the monks had been able to apply themselves so unceasingly to their prodigious labors, which seem beyond the bounds of human endurance.

My work at first was confined to a study of the humanistic volumes in the Laurenziana Library, and the selection of the best examples to be taken as final models for the various letters. From pho-tographed reproductions of selected manuscript pages, I took out fifty examples of each letter. Of these fifty, perhaps a half-dozen would be almost identical, and from these I learned the ex-act design the scribe endeavored to repeat. I also decided to introduce the innovation of having several characters for certain letters that repeated most frequently, in order to preserve the indi-viduality of the hand lettering, and still keep my design within the rigid limitations of type. Of the letter *e,* for instance, eight different designs were

perperam cōſtitutas intellecta ueritate commutatas
corrigi poſſe.Hāc eſſe rem quæ ſi ſemel ſit iudicata
neque alio iudicio commutari:neque ulla poteſtate
corrigi poſſe.Sextus locus eſt per quem conſulto:&
de induſtria factum oſtenditur & illud adiungitur :
uoluntario maleficio ueniam dari non oportere:im-
prudentiæ concedi nonnunq̃ conuenire.Septimus
locus eſt per quē indignamur : quod tetrū : crudele:
nefarium : tyrannicum factum eſſe dicimus p uim:
manū opulētam : quæ res ab legibus:ab æquali iure
remotiſſima ſit.Octauus locus eſt p quē demōſtra-
mus nō uulgare neque factitatū eſſe:neque ab auda-
ciſſimis quidem hominibus id male factum de quo
agit:atq; id a feris hominibus:& a barbaris gētibus
& immanibus beſtiis eſſe remotum.Hæc erunt quæ
ī parentes:liberos:cōiuges.conſāguineos:ſupplices:
crudeliter facta dicuntur:& deinceps ſiqua ̦pferant
in maiores natu:in hoſpites : in uicinos:in amicos :
in eos quibus cū uitā egeris : in eos apud quos edu-
catus ſis : in eos a quibus eruditus:in miſeros mor-
tuos:in miſericordia dignos:in homines claros:no
biles: & honore uſos:in eos qui neque lædere alium
uel defēdere ſe potuerūt:in pueros:ſenes:mulieres:
quibus ex omnibus acriter excitata indignatio:ſum-
mum in eum qui uiolarit horū aliquid odiū cōmo-
uere poterit.Nonus locus eſt per quē cum aliis quæ
cōſtāt eſſe peccata:hoc de quo quæſtio eſt cōparat̄ :
& ita per contentionem quanto atrocius & īdignius
ſit id de quo agitur oſtenditur.Decimus locus eſt p
quem omnia quæ in negocio gerendo acta ſūt quæ

I WHO E'RE WHILE

THE HAPPY GARDEN SUNG,
BY ONE MANS DISOBEDIENCE
LOST, NOW SING
RECOVER'D PARADISE
TO ALL MANKIND,
BY ONE MANS FIRM OBEDIENCE
FULLY TRI'D
THROUGH ALL TEMPTATION,
AND THE TEMPTER FOIL'D
IN ALL HIS WILES,
DEFEATED AND REPULS'T,
AND EDEN RAIS'D
IN THE WAST WILDERNESS.

¶ Thou Spirit who ledst this glorious Eremite
Into the Desert, his Victorious Field
Against the Spiritual Foe, and broughtst him thence
By proof the undoubted Son of God, inspire,
As thou art wont, my prompted Song else mute,
And bear through highth or depth of natures bounds
With prosperous wing full summ'd to tell of deeds
Above Heroic, though in secret done,
And unrecorded left through many an Age,
Worthy t' have not remain'd so long unsung.
¶ Now had the great Proclaimer with a Voice
More awful than the sound of Trumpet, cri'd
Repentance, and Heavens Kingdom nigh at hand
To all Baptiz'd: to his great Baptism flock'd

Emery Walker's Doves Type. From Paradise Regained, *London, 1905* [Exact size]

finally selected; there were five *a*'s, two *m*'s, and so on (see illustration at *page* 32).

After becoming familiar with the individual letters as shown in the Laurenziana humanistic volumes, I went on to Milan and the Ambrosiana Library, with a letter from Doctor Biagi addressed to the librarian, Monsignor Ceriani, explaining the work upon which I was engaged, and seeking his co-operation. It would be impossible to estimate Ceriani's age at that time, but he was very old. He was above middle height, his frame was slight, his eyes penetrating and burning with a fire that showed at a glance how affected he was by the influence to which I have already referred. His skin resembled in color and texture the very parchment of the volumes he handled with such affection, and in his religious habit he seemed the embodiment of ancient learning.

After expressing his deep interest in my undertaking, he turned to a publication upon which he himself was engaged, the reproduction in facsimile of the earliest known manuscript of Homer's *Iliad*. The actual work on this, he explained, was being carried on by his assistant, a younger priest whom he desired to have me meet. His own contribution to the work was an introduction, upon which he was then engaged, and which, he said, was to be

24

his swan song, the final message from his soul to the world.

"This, I suppose, is to be in Italian?" I inquired.

He looked at me reproachfully. "No, my son," he answered, with deep impressiveness; "I am writing my introduction in Latin, which, though called a dead language, will be living long after the present living languages are dead."

Ceriani placed at my disposal the humanistic volumes in the Ambrosiana, and introduced me to his assistant, whose co-operation was of the utmost value in my work. I was particularly struck by the personality of this younger priest. He was in close touch with affairs outside the Church, and asked searching questions regarding conditions in America. He spoke several languages with the same facility with which he spoke his own Italian. His knowledge of books and of bookmaking, past and present, surprised me. All in all, I found him one of the most charming men I have ever met. His name was Achille Ratti, and when he became Bishop of Milan in 1921, and was elevated to the College of Cardinals two months later, I realized how far that wonderful personality was taking him. One could scarcely have foreseen, however, that in less than a year from this time he would become Pope Pius XI.

When, after my drawings were completed, I returned to America, I took up the matter of the type design with Charles Eliot Norton, my old art professor at Harvard, then *emeritus*. Professor Norton was genuinely interested in the whole undertaking, and as the proofs of the various punches later came into my hands he became more and more enthusiastic.

I had arranged to use this type in a series of volumes to be published in London by John Murray, and in America by Little, Brown, and Company. An important question arose as to what should be the first title, and after careful consideration I decided that as Petrarch was the father of humanism his *Trionfi* would obviously be an ideal selection. The volume was to be printed in English rather than in the original Italian, and I settled upon Henry Boyd's translation as the most distinguished.

Upon investigation it developed that the original edition of this book was long out of print and copies were exceedingly rare. The only one I could locate was in the Petrarch collection of the late Willard Fiske. I entered into correspondence with him, and he invited me to be his guest at his villa in Florence. With the type completed, and with proofs in my possession, I undertook my second humanistic Odyssey, making Florence my first objective. Professor Fiske welcomed me cordially, and in him I found a most sympathetic personality, eager to contribute in every way to the success of the undertaking. He placed the volume of Boyd's translation in my hands, and asked that I take it with me for use until my edition was completed.

"This book is unique, and so precious that you certainly could not permit it to go out of your possession," I protested.

His answer was characteristic. "Your love of books," he said, "is such that this volume is as safe in your hands as it is in mine. Take it from me, and return it when it has served its purpose."

Then came the matter of illustrations. In London I had a conference with Sir Sidney Colvin, then Keeper of Prints and Drawings at the British Museum. Colvin had been made familiar with the undertaking by John Murray, who had shown him and Alfred W. Pollard some of the earliest proofs of the punches that I had sent to England. After a careful examination of these, both men suggested to Mr. Murray that his American friend was playing a joke upon him, declaring that the proofs were hand-lettered and not taken from metal originals!

"There is a fate about this," Colvin said, after

I had explained my mission. "We have here in the Museum six original drawings of Petrarch's *Triumphs*, attributed by some to Fra Filippo Lippi and certainly belonging to his school, which have never been reproduced. They are exactly the right size for the *format* which you have determined upon, and if you can have the reproductions made here at the Museum the drawings are at your disposal."

I made arrangements with Emery Walker, the designer of the Doves type and justly famous as an engraver, to etch these plates on steel, and the reproductions of the originals were extraordinarily exact. Those Walker made for the parchment edition looked as if drawn on ivory.

Parchment was required for the specially illu-minated copies which were to form a feature of the edition, and before leaving America I had been told that the Roman grade was the best. I naturally assumed that I should find this in Rome, but my research developed the fact that Roman parch-ment is prepared in Florence. Following this lead, I examined the skins sold by Florentine dealers, but Doctor Biagi assured me that the best grade was not Roman but Florentine, and that Florentine parchment is produced in Issoudun, France. It seemed a far cry to seek out Italian skins in France, but to Issoudun I went. In the meantime I learned that there was a still better grade prepared in Brentford, England — this, in fact, being where William Morris procured the parchment for his Kelmscott publications.

At Brentford I secured my skins; and here I learned something that interested me exceedingly. Owing to the oil which remains in the parchment after it has been prepared for use, the difficulty in printing is almost as great as if on glass. To obviate this, the concern at Brentford, in preparing parch-ment for the Kelmscott volumes, filled in the pores of the skins with chalk, producing an artificial surface. The process of time must operate adversely upon this extraneous substance, and the question naturally arises as to whether eventually, in the Kelmscott parchment volumes, the chalk surface will flake off in spots, producing blemishes which can never be repaired.

For my own purposes I purchased the skins without the artificial surface, and overcame the difficulty in printing by a treatment of the ink which, after much experiment, enabled me to secure as fine results upon the parchment as if printing upon handmade paper.

The volumes were to be printed in the two humanistic colors, black and blue. In the original manuscript volumes this blue is a most unusual shade, the hand letterer having prepared his own ink by grinding *lapis lazuli*, in which there is no red. By artificial light the lines written in blue can scarcely be distinguished from the black. To reproduce the same effect in the printed volume I secured in Florence a limited quantity of *lapis lazuli*, and by special arrangement with the Italian Government had it crushed into powder at the Royal mint. This powder I took home to America, and arranged with a leading manufacturer to produce what I believe to be the first printing ink mixed exactly as the scribes of the fifteenth century used to prepare their pigments.

The months required to produce the *Triumphs* represented a period alternating in anxiety and satisfaction. The greatest difficulty came in impressing upon the typesetter the fact that the various characters of these letters could not be used with mathematical precision, but that the change should come only when he felt his hand would naturally alter the design if he were writing the line instead of setting the type. The experiments required to perfect an ink that should successfully print on the oily parchment were not completed without disappointments and misgivings; the scrupulous care required in reading proofs and

30

its illustrations, so admirable in its presswork, its paper, its binding and its minor accessories.

It does the highest credit to you its originator & to the Press which has so ably seconded your efforts to make it a noble and exemplary work of the Printers' Art.

Your kind words concerning suggestion & encouragement from me remind me of the parable of the Sower. It was the seed that fell into _good_ ground that brought forth fruit.

Believe me, with great regard, and with confident good wishes,

Sincerely Yours

Charles Eliot Norton.

William Dana Orcutt, Esqre

A Page from an Autograph Letter from Charles Eliot Norton

perfecting the spacing, was laborious and monotonous; the scrutinizing of the sheets as they
came from the press was made happier when
the success of the *lapis lazuli* ink was assured.

The rewards came when Professor Norton gave
the volume his unqualified approval—"so interesting and original in its typography and in its
illustrations, so admirable in its presswork, its
paper, its binding, and its minor accessories, .. a
noble and exemplary work of the printers' art";
when George W. Jones, England's artistprinter,
pronounced the Humanistic type "the most beautiful face in the world," and promised to use it in
what he hopes to be his masterpiece, an edition
of Shakespeare's *Sonnets*; when the jury appointed
by the Italian Government to select "the most
beautiful and most appropriate type face to perpetuate the divine Dante" chose the Humanistic
type, and placed the important commission of producing the definitive edition of the great poet, to
commemorate his sexcentenary, in the hands of
that splendid printer, Bertieri, at Milan. Such rewards are not compliments, but justification. Such
beauty as the Humanistic type possesses lies in the
artistic ability and the marvelous skill in execution
of the scribes. My part was simply seizing the development of a period apparently overlooked, and

32

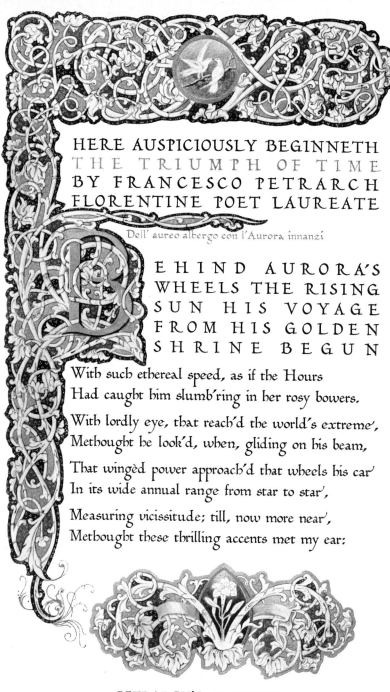

HERE AUSPICIOUSLY BEGINNETH
THE TRIUMPH OF TIME
BY FRANCESCO PETRARCH
FLORENTINE POET LAUREATE

Dell' aureo albergo con l'Aurora innanzi

EHIND AURORA'S
WHEELS THE RISING
SUN HIS VOYAGE
FROM HIS GOLDEN
SHRINE BEGUN

With such ethereal speed, as if the Hours
Had caught him slumb'ring in her rosy bowers.

With lordly eye, that reach'd the world's extreme',
Methought he look'd, when, gliding on his beam,

That wingèd power approach'd that wheels his car'
In its wide annual range from star to star',

Measuring vicissitude; till, now more near',
Methought these thrilling accents met my ear:

PETRARCH'S *TRIUMPHS*
Illuminated Page [10 x 6 inches]
Set in Humanistic Type designed by the Author

IN QUEST OF THE PERFECT BOOK

undertaking the laborious task of translating a
beautiful thing from one medium to another
The Quest of the Perfect Book must necessarily
lead the seeker into far varying roads, the greatest
rewards being found in straying from the main
street into the fascinating bypaths. My quest has
resulted in giving me greater appreciation of the
accomplishments of those who successfully with
stood opposition and persecution in order to make
the printed book a living vehicle to convey the
gems of thought from great minds to the masses,
never forgetful of the value of beauty in its outward
aspect. I believe it possible today to perpetuate the
basic principles of the early artist master-printers
by applying beauty to low-cost books as well as
to limited *éditions de luxe*. The story of the printed
book itself is greater than that contained between
the covers of any single volume, for without it the
history of the world would s___ __ the masses
still plodding on, swathe_ ____ __ _ical
and encyclopædic bo_ ____ ___ the
few would still b_
hoarding the
know_

CHAPTER II
The Kingdom of Books

II

THE KINGDOM OF BOOKS

A PARAPHRASE of, "Would that mine adversary had written a book," might well be, "Would that mine enemy had *printed* a book"; for the building of books has always yielded smaller financial returns for the given amount of labor and ability than is offered in any other line of intelligent human effort.

"Are all the workmen in your establishment blank fools?" an irate publisher demanded of a printer after a particularly aggravating error.

"If they were not," was the patient rejoinder, "they would not be engaged in making books!"

There is an intangible lure that keeps all those associated with the book under subjection. There is a mysterious fascination in being a party to the perpetuation of a human thought that yields something in addition to pecuniary returns. To the author, the inestimable gratification of conveying a message to the world makes him forget the tedious hours of application required before that message can be adequately expressed. To the

37

publisher, the satisfaction of offering the opportunity for occasional genius to come into its own
more than balances the frequent disappointments.
To the book architect, the privilege of supplying the vehicle for thought, and of creating the
physical form of its expression, yields returns not
altogether measurable in coin of the realm.

In 1891, during my apprenticeship at the old
University Press, in Cambridge, Massachusetts,
John Wilson, its famous head, permitted me to
sit in at a conference with Eugene Field and his
friend and admirer, Francis Wilson, the actor,
booklover, and collector. The subject under discussion was the manufacture of a volume of
Field's poems, then called *A New Book of Verses*,
which later became famous under the title of
Second Book of Verse.

Field's personal appearance made a deep impression that first time I saw him. I was then an
undergraduate at Harvard, and this was a live
author at close range! He entered the office with
a peculiar, ambling walk; his clothes were ill-
fitting, accentuating his long legs and arms; his
hands were delicate, with tapering fingers, like
a woman's; his face was pallid; his eyes blue, with
a curiously child-like expression. I remember my

That little bit of a woman's hands

 Reached up into my breast

And rent apart my scoffing heart —

And they buffet it still with such sweet art

 As cannot be expressed.

That little bit of a woman's voice

 Hath grown most wondrous dear;

Above the blare of all elsewhere

(An inspiration that melts at ear)

 It riseth full and clear.

Dear one, I bless the subtle power

 That makes me wholly thine;

And I'm proud to say that I bless the day

When a little woman wrought her way

 Into this life of mine!

— Eugene Field.

feeling of respect, tinged somewhat with awe, as I saw the pages of manuscript spread out upon the table, and listened eagerly to the three-cornered conversation.

In considering the manufacture of his book, Eugene Field had clearly defined ideas of the typographical effect he wished to gain; John Wilson possessed the technical knowledge that enabled him to translate those ideas into terms of type. The examination of the various faces of type, the consideration of the proportions of the page, the selection of the paper, the plan for the design of the cover and the binding,—all came into the discussion.

As I listened, I was conscious of receiving new impressions which gave me a fuller but still incomplete understanding. Until that moment I had found little of interest in the adventure of making books. Now came a realization that the building of a book, like the designing of a house, offered opportunity for *creative* work. This possibility removed the disturbing doubts, and I undertook to discover for myself how that creative element could be crystallized.

Years later came an unexpected echo to the Field episode. After the publication of the *Second Book of Verse*, the manuscript was returned to

Field, who had it bound in half leather and placed it in his library. Upon his death many of his books went by bequest to his life-long friend,

> So come; though I see not his dear little face
>
> And hear not his voice in this jubilant place,
>
> I know he were happy to bid me enshrine
>
> His memory deep in my heart with your play —
>
> Ah me! but a love that is sweeter than mine
>
> Holdeth my boy in its keeping today!
>
> And my heart it is lonely, so, little folk, come,
>
> March in and make merry with trumpet and drum!
>
> — Eugene Field,

Autograph Verse in Eugene Field's Own Copy of Trumpet and Drum

Horace Fletcher, the genial philosopher and famous apostle of dietetics. When Fletcher died, he bequeathed Field's personal volumes to me. By this curious chain of circumstances, thirty-three years after I had seen the manuscript spread out upon the table at the University Press, it came into my possession, bearing the identical memoranda of instruction made upon it by John Wilson, whose large, flowing hand contrasted sharply with the small, copper-plate characters of the author's handwriting.

The present generation of booklovers would think themselves transported back ages rather than decades were they to glance into a great book-printing office of thirty-five years ago. The old University Press at that time acknowledged competition only from the Riverside and the De Vinne Presses, and conditions that obtained there were typical of the times. The business office was called the " counting-room "; the bookkeeper and the head-clerk were perched up on stools at high, sloping desks, and wore long, linen dusters and black skull caps. John Wilson sat at a low table desk, and his partner, who was the financial executive, was the proud possessor of the only roll-top desk in the establishment. Near him, perhaps because of its value as a novelty and thus entitled to the same super-care as the cash, was installed the telephone. Most of the letters were written by Mr. Wilson in his own hand. One of my first responsibilities was to copy these letters on the wetted tissue pages of the copy-book with the turn-screw press.

There was no particular system in effect, and scientific management was unknown. Mr. Wilson used to make out his orders on fragments of paper,—whatever came to hand. When the telephone was first installed he refused to use it, as he

JOHN WILSON IN 1891
Master-Printer

considered this method of conducting business as "sloppy" and even discourteous. To employ a stenographer would have been an evidence of a lazy disposition, and a dictated letter was an offence against dignity and decorum.

A week's work at that time consisted of fifty-nine hours instead of the present forty-eight. Hand composition and electrotyping were figured together as one process and charged at from 80 cents to $1 per thousand ems. Changes required in the type by authors cost 50 cents an hour. An author could afford in those days to rewrite his book after it was in type, but today, with alterations costing five times as much, it is a different proposition!

The wages were as ridiculously low as the prices charged to customers. The girls in the composing room made from $9 to $12 a week, and those receiving the maximum considered themselves potential Hetty Greens. Today, receiving $40 to $45 a week, they find difficulty in making both ends meet. The make-up man, with the "fat" he received in addition to his wage of $16, actually earned about $20 a week, as against $50 to $60 a week now. The foreman of the composing room, with more than two hundred employees under him, received a weekly return of $23, as against $75 to $100 now.

Typsetting, thirty-five years ago, was almost entirely by hand, as this was before the day of the linotype and the monotype. Thorne typesetting machines, which then seemed marvels of mechanical ingenuity, failed to prove economical because they required two operatives and so easily got out of order. The composing room itself was laid out with its main avenues and side streets like a well-ordered town, divisions being marked by the frames bearing the cases of type in various faces and sizes. The correcting stones ran down the center.

The foreman of the composing room was the king of his domain and a power unto himself. Each side street was an " alley," in which from four to eight typesetters worked, back to back. These were sometimes boys or men, but usually girls or women. The " crew " in each alley was in charge of an experienced typesetter. It was he who received from the foreman the manuscript to be put into type; who distributed the copy, a few pages at a time to each of his subordinates; who supervised the work, and arranged for the galleys to be collated in their proper order for proofing; and who was generally responsible for

44

the product of his alley. As was characteristic
of the times in well-conducted industrial plants,
the workers in this department, as in the others,
were simply a large family presided over by the
foreman, who interpreted the instructions from
the management; and by the heads of the crews,
who carried out the detailed instructions of the
foreman.

There was a pride in workmanship that is
mostly lacking in manufacturing plants today,
due largely to the introduction of labor-saving
machinery, and again to the introduction of efficiency methods. Both were inevitable, but the
price paid for the gain in production was high. I
am old-fashioned enough to hope that modern
ideas of efficiency will never be applied in the printing industry to the extent of robbing the workman of his individuality. Books are such personal
things! I am in full sympathy with that efficiency
which cuts out duplication of effort. I believe in
studying methods of performing each operation
to discover which one is the most economical in
time and effort. I realize that in great manufacturing plants, where machines have replaced so
largely the work of the human hand, it is obviously
necessary for workmen to spend their days manufacturing only a part of the complete article; but

45

when the organization of any business goes so far as to substitute numbers for names I feel that something has been destroyed, and that in taking away his individuality from the workman the work suffers the same loss.

I have even asked myself whether the greatest underlying cause of strikes and labor disturbances during the past ten years has not been the unrest that has come to the workman because he can no longer take actual pride in the product of his hand. Years ago, after the death of one of my oldest employees, I called upon his widow, and in the simple " parlor " of the house where he had lived, prominently placed on a marble-top table as the chief ornament in the room, lay a copy of Wentworth's " Geometry." When I picked it up the widow said proudly, " Jim set every page of that book with his own hands." It was a priceless heirloom in which the workman's family took continued and justifiable pride.

The old University Press family was not only happy but loyal. When the business found itself in financial difficulties, owing to outside speculations by Mr. Wilson's partner, the workmen brought their bankbooks, with deposits amounting to over twenty thousand dollars, and laid them on Mr. Wilson's desk, asking him to use these funds in whatever way he chose. The sum involved was infinitesimal compared to the necessities, but the proffer was a human gesture not calculable in financial digits.

Proofreading was an art in the eighteen-nineties instead of an annoying necessity, as it now seems to be considered. The chief readers were highly educated men and women, some having been clergymen or schoolteachers. One proofreader at the University Press at that time could read fourteen languages, and all the readers were competent to discuss with the authors points that came up in the proof. The proof was read, not only to discover typographical errors, but also to query dates, quotations, and even statements of fact. Well-known authors were constantly running in and out of the Press, frequently going directly to the proofreaders, and sometimes even to the compositors themselves, without coming in touch with the counting-room. Mr. Wilson looked upon the authors and publishers as members of his big family, and "No Admittance" signs were conspicuous by their absence.

The modern practice of proofreading cannot produce as perfect volumes as resulted from the deliberate, painstaking, and time-consuming consideration which the old-time proofreaders gave to every book passing through their hands. Today the proof is read once, and then revised and sent out to the author. When made up into page form and sent to foundry it is again revised, but not re-read. No proof used to go out from a first-class printing office without a first and a second reading by copy. It was then read a third time by a careful foundry reader before being made into plates. Unfortunately, with labor at its present cost, no publisher could produce a volume at a price that the public would pay, if the old-time care were devoted to its manufacture.

Time was when a reputation for careful proofreading was an asset to a Press. One day the office boy came to my private office and said that there was a man downstairs who insisted upon seeing me personally, but who declined to give his name. From the expression on the boy's face I concluded that the visitor must be a somewhat unique character, and I was not disappointed.

As he came into my office he had every aspect of having stepped off the vaudeville stage. He had on the loose garments of a farmer, with the broad hat that is donned only on state occasions.

He wore leather boots over which were rubbers, and carried a huge, green umbrella.

He nodded pleasantly as he came in, and sat down with great deliberation. Before making any remarks he laid his umbrella on the floor and placed his hat carefully over it, then he somewhat painfully removed his rubbers. This done, he turned to me with a broad smile of greeting, and said, "I don't know as you know who I am."

When I confirmed him in his suspicions, he remarked, " Well, I am Jasper P. Smith, and I come from Randolph, New Hampshire."

(*The names and places mentioned are, for obvious reasons, not correct.*)

I returned his smile of greeting and asked what I could do for him.

"Well," he said, "my home town of Randolph, New Hampshire, has decided to get out a town history, and I want to have you do the printin' of it. The selectmen thought it could be printed at———, but I says to them, 'If it's worth doin' at all it's worth doin' right, and I want the book to be made at the University Press in Cambridge.'"

I thanked Mr. Smith for his confidence, and expressed my satisfaction that our reputation had reached Randolph, New Hampshire.

"Well," he said, chuckling to himself, " you

see, it was this way. You made the history of Rumford, and I was the feller who wrote the genealogies. That's what I am, a genealogy feller. Nobody in New Hampshire can write a town history without comin' to me for genealogies."

After pausing for a moment he continued, " It was your proofreadin' that caught me. On that Rumford book your proofreader was a smart one, she was, but I got back at her in good style."

His memory seemed to cause him considerable amusement, and I waited expectantly.

" It was in one of the genealogies," he went on finally. " I gave the date of the marriage as so and so, and the date of the birth of the first child as two months later. Did she let that go by? I should say not. She drew a line right out into the margin and made a darned big question mark. But I got back at her! I just left that question mark where it was, and wrote underneath, ' Morally incorrect, historically correct! ' "

When the first Adams flat-bed press was installed at the University Press, President Felton of Harvard College insisted that no book of his should ever be printed upon this modern monstrosity. Here was history repeating itself, for book-lovers of the fifteenth century in Italy for a long

time refused to admit that a printed volume had
its place in a gentleman's library. In the eighteen-
nineties one whole department at the University
Press consisted of these flat-bed presses, which
today can scarcely be found outside of museums.
If a modern publisher were to stray into the old
loft where the wetted sheets from these presses
were hung over wooden rafters to dry, he would
rub his eyes and wonder in what age he was living.
The paper had been passed through tubs of water,
perhaps half a quire at a time, and partially dried
before being run through the press. The old
Adams presses made an impression that could
have been read by the blind, and all this emboss-
ing, together with the wrinkling of the sheet
from the moisture, had to be taken out under
hydraulic pressure. Today wetted sheets and the
use of hydraulic presses for bookwork are practically obsolete. The cylinder presses, that run twice
as fast, produce work of equal quality at lower
cost.

In those days the relations between publishers
and their printers were much more intimate.
Scales of prices were established from time to
time, but a publisher usually sent all his work to
the same printer. It was also far more customary

for a publisher to send an author to the printer to discuss questions of typography with the actual maker of the book, or to argue some technical or structural point in his manuscript with the head proofreader. The headreader in a large printing establishment at that time was a distinct personality, quite competent to meet authors upon their own ground.

One of my earliest and pleasantest responsibilities was to act as Mr. Wilson's representative in his business relations with Mrs. Mary Baker Eddy, which required frequent trips to "Pleasant View" at Concord, New Hampshire. Mrs. Eddy always felt under deep obligation to Mr. Wilson for his interest in the manuscript of *Science and Health* when she first took it to him with a view to publication, and any message from him always received immediate and friendly consideration.

In the past there have been suggestions made that the Rev. James Henry Wiggin, a retired Unitarian clergyman and long a proofreader at the University Press, rewrote *Science and Health*. Mr. Wiggin was still proofreader when I entered the Press, and he always manifested great pride in having been associated with Mrs. Eddy in the revision of this famous book. I often heard the matter referred to, both by him and by John Wilson, but there never was the slightest intimation that Mr. Wiggin's services passed beyond those of an experienced editor. I have no doubt that many of his suggestions, in his editorial capacity, were of value and possibly accepted by the author,—in fact, unless they had been, he would not have exercised his proper function; but had he contributed to the new edition what some have claimed, he would certainly have given intimation of it in his conversations with me.

The characteristic about Mrs. Eddy that impressed me the first time I met her was her motherliness. She gave every one the impression of deepest interest and concern in what he said, and was sympathetic in everything that touched on his personal affairs. When I told her of John Wilson's financial calamity, she seemed to regard it as a misfortune of her own. Before I left her that day she drew a check for a substantial sum and offered it to me.

"Please hand that to my old friend," she said, "and tell him to be of good cheer. What he has given of himself to others all these years will now return to him a thousand-fold."

At first one might have been deceived by her quiet manner into thinking that she was easily influenced. There was no suggestion to which she did not hold herself open. If she approved, she accepted it promptly; if it did not appeal, she dismissed it with a graciousness that left no mark; but it was always settled once and for all. There was no wavering and no uncertainty.

After Mrs. Eddy moved from Concord to Boston, her affairs were administered by her Trustees, so I saw her less frequently. To many her name suggests a great religious movement, but when I think of her I seem to see acres of green grass, a placid little lake, a silver strip of river, and a boundary line of hills; and within the unpretentious house a slight, unassuming woman,—very real, very human, very appealing, supremely content in the self-knowledge that, no matter what others might think, she was delivering her message to the world.

By this time, I had discovered what was the matter with American bookmaking. It was a contracting business, and books were conceived and made by the combined efforts of the publisher, the manufacturing man, the artist, the decorator, the paper mills' agent, and, last of all, the printer and the binder. This was not the way the old-time printers had planned their books. With all their mechanical limitations, they had followed architectural lines kept consistent and harmonious because controlled by a single mind, while the finished volume of the eighteen-nineties was a composite production of many minds, with no architectural plan. No wonder that the volumes manufactured, even in the most famous Presses, failed to compare with those produced in Venice by Jenson and Aldus four centuries earlier!

When I succeeded John Wilson as head of the University Press in 1895, I determined to carry out the resolution I had formed four years earlier, while sitting in on the Eugene Field conference, of following the example of the early master-printers so far as this could be done amidst modern conditions. Some of my publisher friends were partially convinced by my contention that if the printer properly fulfilled his function he must know how to express his clients' mental conception of the physical attributes of prospective volumes in terms of type, paper, presswork, and binding better than they could do it themselves. The Kelmscott publications, which appeared at this time, were of great value in emphasizing my contention, for William Morris placed printing back among the fine arts after it had lapsed into a trade.

I had no idea, when I presented my plan, of persuading my friends to produce typographical monuments. No demand has ever existed for volumes of this type adequate to the excessive cost involved by the perfection of materials, the accuracy of editorial detail, the supreme excellence of typography and presswork, and the glory of the binding. Sweynheim and Pannartz, Gutenberg's successors, were ruined by their experiments in Greek; the Aldine Press in Venice was saved only by the intervention of Jean Grolier; Henri Étienne was ruined by his famous *Thesaurus,* and Christophe Plantin would have been bankrupted by his *Polyglot Bible* had he not retrieved his fortunes by later and meaner publications. Nor was I unmindful of similar examples that might have been cited from more modern efforts, made by ambitious publishers and printers.

What I wanted to do was to build low-cost volumes upon the same principles as *de luxe* editions, eliminating the expensive materials but retaining the harmony and consistency that come from designing the book from an architectural standpoint. It adds little to the expense to select a type that properly expresses the thought which the author wishes to convey; or to have the presses touch the letters into the paper in such a way as to

56

become a part of it, without that heavy impression which makes the reverse side appear like an example of Braille; or to find a paper (even made by machine!) soft to the feel and grateful to the eye, on which the page is placed with well-considered margins; or to use illustrations or decorations, if warranted at all, in such a way as to assist the imagination of the reader rather than to divert him from the text; to plan a title page which, like the door to a house, invites the reader to open it and proceed, its type lines carefully balanced with the blank; or to bind (even in cloth!) with trig squares and with design or lettering in keeping with the printing inside.

By degrees the publishers began to realize that this could be done, and when once established, the idea of treating the making of books as a manufacturing problem instead of as a series of contracts with different concerns, no one of which knew what the others were doing, found favor. The authors also preferred it, for their literary children now went forth to the world in more becoming dress. Thus serving in the capacity of book architect and typographical advisor, instead of merely as a contracting printer, these years have been lived in a veritable Kingdom of Books, in company with interesting people,—authors and artists as

57

well as publishers,— in a delightfully intimate way because I have been permitted to be a part of the great adventure.

During these years I have seen dramatic changes. Wages were somewhat advanced between 1891 and the outbreak of the World War, but even at this latter date the cost of manufacturing books was less than half of what it is now. This is the great problem which publishers have to face today. When the cost of everything doubled after the World War, the public accepted the necessity of paying twice the price for a theater ticket as a matter of course; but when the retail price of books was advanced in proportion to the cost of manufacture, there was a great outcry among buyers that authors, publishers, and booksellers were opportunists, demanding an unwarranted profit. As a matter of fact, the novel which used to sell at $1.35 per copy should now sell at $2.50 if the increased costs were properly apportioned. The publisher today is forced to decline many promising first novels because the small margin of profit demands a comparatively large first edition. Unless a publisher can sell 5,000 copies as a minimum it is impossible for him to make any profit upon a novel. Taking this as a basis, and a novel as containing 320 pages, suppose we see how the $2.00 retail price distributes itself. The cost of manufacture, including the typesetting, electrotype plates, cover design, jacket, brass dies, presswork, paper, and binding, amounts to 42 cents per copy (in England, about 37 cents). The publisher's cost of running his office, which he calls "overhead," is 36 cents per copy. The minimum royalty received by an author is 10 per cent. of the retail price, which would give him 20 cents. This makes a total cost of 98 cents a copy, without advertising. But a book must be advertised.

A $2.00 book is sold by the publisher to the retail bookseller for $1.20, and the bookseller figures that his cost of doing business is one third, or 40 cents. This, then, shows a gross profit to the publisher of 22 cents a copy, to the retail bookseller of 40 cents, and to the author of 20 cents a copy.

The net profit is considerably less. A book requires advertising, and every $50 spent in this way adds a cent a copy to the publisher's cost. The free copies distributed for press reviews represent no trifling item. A thousand dollars is not a large amount to be spent for advertising, and this means 20 cents a copy on a 5,000 edition, reducing the publisher's profit to 2 cents.

Beyond this, there is an additional expense to both bookseller and publisher which the buyer of books is likely to overlook. It is impossible to know just when the demand for a book will cease, and this means that the publisher and the book-seller are frequently left with copies on hand which have to be disposed of at a price below cost. This is an expense that has to be included in the book business just as much as in handling fruit, flowers, or other perishable goods.

When a publisher is able to figure on a large demand for the first edition, he can cut down the cost of manufacture materially; but, on the other hand, this is at least partially offset by the fact that authors whose books warrant large first editions demand considerably more than 10 per cent. royalty, and the advertising item on a big seller runs into large figures.

I wish I might say that I had seen a dramatic change in the methods employed in the retail bookstores! There still exists, with a few notable exceptions, the same lack of realization that familiarity with the goods one has to sell is as necessary in merchandizing books as with any other commodity. Salesmen in many otherwise well-organized retail bookstores are still painfully ignorant of their proper functions and indifferent to the legitimate requirements of their prospective customers.

Some years ago, when one of my novels was having its run, I happened to be in New York at a time when a friend was sailing for Europe. He had announced his intention of purchasing a copy of my book to read on the steamer, and I asked him to permit me to send it to him with the author's compliments. Lest any reader be astonished to learn that an author ever buys a copy of his own book, let me record the fact that except for the twelve which form a part of his contract with the publisher, he pays cash for every copy he gives away. Mark Twain dedicated the first edition of *The Jumping Frog* to "John Smith." In the second edition he omitted the dedication, explaining that in dedicating the volume as he did, he had felt sure that at least all the John Smiths would buy books. To his consternation he found that they all expected complimentary copies, and he was hoist by his own petard!

With the idea of carrying out my promise to my friend, I stepped into one of the largest bookstores in New York, and approached a clerk, asking him for the book by title. My pride was somewhat hurt to find that even the name was entirely unfamiliar to him. He ran over various volumes upon the counter, and then turned to me, saying, "We don't carry that book, but we have several others here which I am sure you would like better."

"Undoubtedly you have," I agreed with him; "but that is beside the point. I am the author of the book I asked for, and I wish to secure a copy to give to a friend. I am surprised that a store like this does not carry it."

Leaning nonchalantly on a large, circular pile of books near him, the clerk took upon himself the education of the author.

"It would require a store much larger than this to carry every book that is published, wouldn't it?" he asked cheerfully. "Of course each au- thor naturally thinks his book should have the place of honor on the bookstalls, but we have to be governed by the demand."

It was humiliating to learn the real reason why this house failed to carry my book. I had to say something to explain my presumption even in assuming that I might find it there, so in my confusion I stammered,

"But I understood from the publishers that the book was selling very well."

"Oh, yes," the clerk replied indulgently; "they

have to say that to their authors to keep them satisfied! "

With the matter thus definitely settled, nothing remained but to make my escape as gracefully as circumstances would permit. As I started to leave, the clerk resumed his standing position, and my eye happened to rest on the pile of perhaps two hundred books upon which he had been half-reclining. The jacket was strikingly familiar. Turning to the clerk I said severely,

" Would you mind glancing at that pile of books from which you have just risen? "

" Oh! " he exclaimed, smiling and handing me a copy, " that is the very book we were looking for, isn't it? "

It seemed my opportunity to become the educator, and I seized it.

" Young man," I said, " if you would discontinue the practice of letting my books support you, and sell a few copies so that they might support me, it would be a whole lot better for both of us."

" Ha, ha! " he laughed, graciously pleased with my sally; " that's a good line, isn't it? I really must read your book! "

The old-time publisher is passing, and the author is largely to blame. I have seen the close association—in many cases the profound friend-ship—between author and publisher broken by the commercialism fostered by some literary agents and completed by competitive bids made by one publishing house to beguile a popular author away from another. There was a time when a writer was proud to be classified as a " Macmillan," or a " Harper " author. He felt himself a part of the publisher's organization, and had no hesita-tion in taking his literary problems to the editorial advisor of the house whose imprint appeared upon the title pages of his volumes. A celebrated Boston authoress once found herself absolutely at a standstill on a partially completed novel. She confided her dilemma to her publisher, who immediately sent one of his editorial staff to the rescue. They spent two weeks working together over the manuscript, solved the problems, and the novel, when published, was the most successful of the season.

Several publishers have acknowledged to me that in offering unusually high royalties to authors they have no expectation of breaking even, but that to have a popular title upon their list in-creases the sales of their entire line. The publisher from whom the popular writer is filched has usually done his share in helping him attain his popularity. The royalty he pays is a fair division of the profits. He cannot, in justice to his other authors, pay him a further premium.

Ethics, perhaps, has no place in business, but the relation between author and publisher seems to me to be beyond a business covenant. A pub⁄lisher may deliberately add an author to his list at a loss in order to accomplish a specific purpose, but this practice cannot be continued indefinitely. A far⁄sighted author will consider the matter seri⁄ously before he becomes an opportunist.

In England this questionable practice has been of much slower growth. The House of Murray, in London, is one of those still conducted on the old⁄time basis. John Murray IV, the present head of the business, has no interest in any author who comes to him for any reason other than a desire to have the Murray imprint upon his book. It is more than a business. The publishing offices at 50a, Albemarle Street adjoin and open out of the Murray home. In the library is still shown the fireplace where John Murray III burned Byron's letters, after purchasing them at an enormous price, because he deemed that their publication would do injury to the reputation of the writer and of the House itself.

John Murray II was one of the publishers of Scott's *Marmion*. In those days it was customary for publishers to share their contracts. Constable had purchased from Scott for £1,000 the copyright of *Marmion* without having seen a single line, and the *honorarium* was paid the author before the poem was completed or the manuscript delivered. Constable, however, promptly disposed of a one-fourth interest to Mr. Miller of Albemarle Street, and another one fourth to John Murray, then of Fleet Street.

By 1829 Scott had succeeded in getting into his own hands nearly all his copyrights, one of the outstanding items being this one-quarter interest in *Marmion* held by Mr. Murray. Longmans and Constable had tried in vain to purchase it. When, however, Scott himself approached Murray through Lockhart, the following letter from Mr. Murray was the result:

So highly do I estimate the honour of being even in so small a degree the publisher of the author of the poem that no pecuniary consideration whatever can induce me to part with it. But there is a consideration of another kind that would make it painful to me if I were to retain it a moment longer. I mean the knowledge of its being required by the author, into whose hands it was spontaneously resigned at the same instant that I read the request.

THE KINGDOM OF BOOKS

There has always been a vast difference in authors in the attitude they assume toward the transformation of their manuscripts into printed books. Most of them leave every detail to their publishers, but a few take a deep and intelligent personal interest. Bernard Shaw is to be included in the latter group.

A leading Boston publisher once telephoned me that an unknown English author had submitted a manuscript for publication, but that it was too socialistic in its nature to be acceptable. Then the publisher added that the author had asked, in case this house did not care to publish the volume, that arrangements be made to have the book printed in this country in order to secure American copyright.

" We don't care to have anything to do with it," was the statement; " but I thought perhaps you might like to manufacture the book."

" Who is the author? " I inquired.

" It's a man named Shaw."

" What is the rest of his name? "

" Wait a minute and I'll find out."

Leaving the telephone for a moment, the publisher returned and said,

" His name is G. Bernard Shaw. Did you ever hear of him? "

"Yes," I replied; "I met him laſt summer in London through Cobden-Sanderson, and I should be glad to undertake the manufacture of the book for Mr. Shaw."

"All right," came the answer. "Have your boy call for the manuscript."

This manuscript was *Man and Superman*.

From that day and for many years, Shaw and I carried on a desultory correspondence, his letters proving moſt original and diverting. On one occasion he took me severely to task for having used two sizes of type upon a title page. He wrote four pages to prove what poor taſte and work-manship this represented, and then ended the letter with these words, "But, after all, any other printer would have used sixteen inſtead of two, so I bless you for your reſtraint!"

We had another lengthy discussion on the use of apoſtrophes in printing. "I have made no at-tempt to deal with the apoſtrophes you introduce," he wrote; "but my own usage is carefully con-sidered and the inconsiſtencies are only apparent. For inſtance, *Ive, youve, lets, thats,* are quite un-miſtakable, but *Ill, hell, shell,* for *I'll, he'll, she'll,* are impossible without a phonetic alphabet to distinguish between long and short *e*. In such cases I retain the apoſtrophe, in all others I discard it. Now you may ask me why I discard it. Solely because it spoils the printing. If you print a Bible you can make a handsome job of it because there are no apostrophes or inverted commas to break up the letterpress with holes and dots. Until people are forced to have some consideration for a book as something to look at as well as something to read, we shall never get rid of these senseless disfigurements that have destroyed all the old sense of beauty in printing."

" Ninety-nine per cent. of the secret of good printing," Shaw continued, " is not to have patches of white or trickling rivers of it trailing down a page, like rain-drops on a window. Horrible! *White* is the enemy of the printer. *Black,* rich, fat, even black, without gray patches, is, or should be, his pride. Leads and quads and displays of different kinds of type should be reserved for insurance prospectuses and advertisements of lost dogs. . . ."

His enthusiasm for William Morris' leaf ornaments is not shared by all booklovers. Glance at any of the Kelmscott volumes, and you will find these glorified oak leaves scattered over the type page in absolutely unrelated fashion,—a greater blemish, to some eyes, than occasional variation in spacing. Shaw writes:

If you look at one of the books printed by William Morris, the greatest printer of the XIX century, and one of the greatest printers of all the centuries, you will see that he occasionally puts in a little leaf ornament, or something of the kind. The idiots in America who tried to imitate Morris, not understanding this, peppered such things all over their "art" books, and generally managed to stick in an extra large quad before each to show how little they understood about the business. Morris doesn't do this in his own books. He rewrites the sentence so as to make it justify, without bringing one gap underneath another in the line above. But in printing other people's books, which he had no right to alter, he sometimes found it impossible to avoid this. Then, sooner than spoil the rich, even color of his block of letter-press by a big white hole, he filled it up with a leaf.

Do not dismiss this as not being "business." I assure you, I have a book which Morris gave me, a single copy, by selling which I could cover the entire cost of printing my books, and its value is due solely to its having been manufactured in the way I advocate; there's absolutely no other secret about it; and there is no reason why you should not make yourself famous through all the ages by turning out editions of standard works on these lines whilst other printers are exhausting themselves in dirty felt end papers, sham Kelmscott capitals, leaf ornaments in quad sauce, and then wondering why nobody in Europe will pay twopence for them, whilst Kelmscott books and Doves Press books of Morris'

THE KINGDOM OF BOOKS

friends, Emery Walker and Cobden-Sanderson, fetch fancy
prices before the ink is thoroughly dry . . . .
After this I shall have to get you to print all my
future books, so please have this treatise
printed in letters of gold and
preserved for future
reference

CHAPTER III
Friends through Type

III

FRIENDS THROUGH TYPE

IN 1903 I again visited Italy to continue my study of the art of printing in the old monasteries and libraries, sailing on the S. S. *Canopic* from Boston to Naples. Among the passengers on board I met Horace Fletcher, returning to his home in Venice. At that time his volume *Menticulture* was having a tremendous run. I had enjoyed reading the book, and in its author I discovered a unique and charming personality; in fact, I have never met so perfect an expression of practical optimism. His humor was infectious, his philosophy appealing, his quiet persistency irresistible.

To many people the name of Horace Fletcher has become associated with the Gladstonian doctrine of excessive chewing, but this falls far short of the whole truth. His scheme was the broadest imaginable, and thorough mastication was only the hub into which the other spokes of the wheel of his philosophy of life were to be fitted. The scheme was nothing less than a cultivation of progressive human efficiency. Believing that absolute health is the real basis of human happiness and advancement, and that health depends upon an intelligent treatment of food in the mouth together with knowledge of how best to furnish the fuel that is actually required to run the human engine, Horace Fletcher sought for and found perfect guides among the natural human instincts and physiologic facilities, and demonstrated that his theories were facts.

During the years that followed I served as his typographic mentor. He was eager to try weird and ingenious experiments to bring out the various points of his theories through unique typographi- cal arrangement (see *opp. page*). It required all my skill and diplomacy to convince him that type possessed rigid limitations, and that to gain his emphasis he must adopt less complicated methods. From this association we became the closest of friends, and presuming upon this relation I used to banter him upon being so casual. His copy was never ready when the compositors needed it; he was always late in returning his proofs. The manufacture of a Fletcher book was a hectic ex- perience, yet no one ever seemed to take exceptions. This was characteristic of the man. He moved and acted upon suddenly formed impulses, never

The Real Remedy

Don't eat when not hungry
Don't ever get angry
Don't drink in a hurry
Don't tolerate worry
Don't ever waste good taste
Don't pass it by in haste
Don't gobble pure good food
Don't fail to feed as should
Don't make work of exercise
Don't make light of good advice
Don't ever half take breath
Don't thus court an early death
Don't doubt Divine Design
Don't squander precious time
Don't miss to do your best
Let Nature do the rest

Only ten of these easy "Donts" (one for each of his ten digits) is man's share of care in his partnership with Natural Growth. Unobstructed Growth will do all necessary to fully satisfy the needs of Success, Altruism and Happiness

Horace Fletcher

A Page of Horace Fletcher Manuscript

planning ahead yet always securing exactly what he wanted, and those inconvenienced the most always seemed to enjoy it.

"I believe," he used to say, "in hitching one's wagon to a star, but I always keep my bag packed and close at hand ready to change stars at a moment's notice. It is only by doing this that you can give things a chance to happen to you."

Among the volumes Fletcher had with him on board ship was one he had purchased in Italy, printed in a type I did not recognize but which greatly attracted me by its beauty. The book bore the imprint: *Parma: Co'tipi Bodoniani.* Some weeks later, in a small, second-hand bookstore in Florence, I happened upon a volume printed in the same type, which I purchased and took at once to my friend, Doctor Guido Biagi, at the Laurenziana Library.

"The work of Giambattista Bodoni is not familiar to you?" he inquired in surprise. "It is he who revived in Italy the glory of the Aldi. He and Firmin Didot in Paris were the fathers of modern type design at the beginning of the nineteenth century."

"Is this type still in use?" I inquired.

"No," Biagi answered. "When Bodoni died there was no one worthy to continue its use, so

78

GIAMBATTISTA BODONI, 1740-1813
From Engraving at the Bibliothèque Nationale, Paris

his matrices and punches are kept intact, exactly as he left them. They are on exhibition in the library at Parma, just as the old Plantin relics are preserved in the museum at Antwerp."

I immediately took steps through our Ambassador at Rome to gain permission from the Italian Government to recut this face for use in America. After considerable difficulty and delay this permission was granted, with a proviso that I should not allow any of the type made from my proposed matrices to get into the hands of Italian printers, as this would detract from the prestige of the city of Parma. It was a condition to which I was quite willing to subscribe! Within a year I have received a prospectus from a revived Bodoni Press at Montagnola di Lugano, Switzerland, announcing that the exclusive use of the original types of Giambattista Bodoni has been given them by the Italian Government. This would seem to indicate that the early governmental objections have disappeared.

While searching around to secure the fullest set of patterns, I stumbled upon the fact that Bodoni and Didot had based their types upon the same model, and that Didot had made use of his font particularly in the wonderful editions published in Paris at the very beginning of the nineteenth

79

century. I then hurried to Paris to see whether these matrices were in existence. There, after a search through the foundries, I discovered the original punches, long discarded, in the foundry of Peignot, to whom I gave an order to cast the different sizes of type, which I had shipped to America.

This was the first type based on this model ever to come into this country. The Bodoni face has since been recut by typefounders as well as for the typesetting machines, and is today one of the most popular faces in common use. Personally I prefer the Bodoni letter to that of Didot (see *opp.page*). The Frenchman succumbed to the elegance of his period, and by lightening the thin lines robbed the design of the virility that Bodoni retained. I am not in sympathy with the excessive height of the ascending letters, which frequently extend beyond the capitals; but when one considers how radical a departure from precedent this type was, he must admire the skill and courage of the designers. William Morris cared little for it,—" The sweltering hideousness of the Bodoni letter," he exclaimed; " the most illegible type that was ever cut, with its preposterous thicks and thins "; while Theodore L. De Vinne, in his *Practice of Typography*, writes:

80

Allons aux Grecs livrer le fils d'Hector.

ANDROMAQUE, *se jetant aux pieds de Pyrrhus.*

Ah, seigneur! arrêtez! que prétendez-vous faire?
Si vous livrez le fils, livrez-leur donc la mere!
Vos serments m'ont tantòt juré tant d'amitié!
Dieux! ne pourrai-je au moins toucher votre pitié?
Sans espoir de pardon m'avez-vous condamnée?

Cortona, *petite, et ancienne ville d'Italie en Toscane dans le Florentin avec un Evéché Suf. de Florence et une célebre Académie. C'est la patrie de Pierre Berretin, fameux peintre du siecle passé.*

Cortona, città d'Italia nella Toscana, la quale ha Vescovado ed una celebre Accademia, da cui escono soventi dissertazioni dotte ed erudite. Il famoso pittore Pietro Berettini ebbe quivi i natali.

The Bodoni Letter [bottom] *compared with the Didot Letter* [top]

IN QUEST OF THE PERFECT BOOK

The beauty of the Bodoni letters consists in their regularity, in their clearness, and in their conformity to the taste of the race, nation, and age in which the work was first written, and finally in the grace of the characters, independent of time or place.

When authorities differ to such a wide extent, the student of type design must draw his own conclusions!

Fletcher's idea of an appointment was something to be kept if or when convenient, yet he never seemed to offend any one. He did nothing he did not wish to do, and his methods of extricating himself from unwelcome responsibilities always amused rather than annoyed. "If you don't want to do a thing very badly," he confided to me on one such occasion, "do it very badly."

On board the *Canopic* Fletcher was surrounded by an admiring and interested group. General Leonard Wood was on his way to study colonial government abroad before taking up his first administration as Governor of the Philippines. On his staff was General Hugh Lennox Scott, who later succeeded General Wood as Chief of Staff of the United States Army. The conversations and discussions in the smokeroom each evening

HORACE FLETCHER IN 1915

after dinner were illuminating and fascinating. General Wood had but recently completed his work as Governor of Cuba, and he talked freely of his experiences there, while General Scott was full of reminiscences of his extraordinary adventures with the Indians. He later played an important part in bringing peace to the Philippines.

It was at one of these four-cornered sessions in the smokeroom that we first learned of Fletcher's ambition to revolutionize the world in its methods of eating. That he would actually accomplish this no one of us believed, but the fact remains. The smokeroom steward was serving the coffee, inquiring of each one how many lumps of sugar he required. Fletcher, to our amazement, called for five! It was a grand-stand play in a way, but he secured his audience as completely as do the tambourines and the singing of the Salvation Army.

" Why are you surprised? " he demanded with seeming innocence. " I am simply taking a coffee liqueur, in which there is less sugar now than there is in your chartreuse or benedictine. But I am mixing it with the saliva, which is more than you are doing. The sugar, as you take it, becomes acid in the stomach and retards digestion; by my

83

method, it is changed into grape sugar, which is easily assimilated."

"To insalivate one's liquor," he explained to us, "gives one the most exquisite pleasure imaginable, but it is a terrific test of quality. It brings out the richness of flavor, which is lost when one gulps the wine down. Did you ever notice the way a tea-taster sips his tea?"

As he talked he exposed the ignorance of the entire group on physiological matters to an embarrassing extent, clinching his remarks by asking General Wood the question,

"Would you engage as chauffeur for your automobile a man who knew as little about his motor as you know about your own human engine?"

No one ever loved a practical joke better than Horace Fletcher. I was a guest at a dinner he once gave at the Graduates' Club in New Haven. Among the others present were President Hadley of Yale, John Hays Hammond, Walter Camp, and Professor Lounsbury. There was considerable curiosity and some speculation concerning what would constitute a Fletcher dinner. At the proper time we were shown into a private room, where the table was set with the severest simplicity. Instead of china, white crockery was used, and the chief table-decorations were three large crockery pitchers filled with ice water. At each plate was a crockery saucer, containing a shredded-wheat biscuit. It was amusing to glance around and note the expressions of dismay upon the faces of the guests. Their worst apprehensions were being confirmed! Just as we were well seated, the headwaiter came to the door and announced that by mistake we had been shown into the wrong room, whereupon Fletcher, with an inimitable twinkle in his eye, led the way into another private dining-room, where we sat down to one of the most sumptuous repasts I have ever enjoyed.

Today, twenty years after his campaign, it is almost forgotten that the American breakfast was at that time a heavy meal. Horace Fletcher revolutionized the practice of eating, and interjected the word *fletcherize* into the English language. As a disciple of Fletcher Sir Thomas Barlow, physician-in-chief to King Edward VII, persuaded royalty to set the style by cutting down the formal dinner from three hours to an hour and a half, with a corresponding relief to the digestive apparatus of the guests. In Belgium, during the World War, working with Herbert Hoover, Fletcher taught the impoverished people how to sustain themselves upon meager rations. Among his admirers and devoted friends were such profound

85

thinkers as William James who, in response to a letter from him, wrote, " Your excessive reaction to the stimulus of my grateful approval makes you remind me of those rich soils which, when you tickle them with a straw, smile with a harvest "; and Henry James, who closes a letter: " Come and bring with you plenary absolution to the thankless subject who yet dares light the lamp of gratitude to you at each day's end of his life."

My acquaintance with Henry James came through my close association with the late Sir Sidney Lee, the Shakesperian authority, and Horace Fletcher.

" Don't be surprised if he is brusque or un-civil," Sir Sidney whispered to me just before I met him at dinner; " one can never tell how he is going to act."

As a matter of fact, I found Henry James a most genial and enjoyable dinner companion, and never, during the few later occasions when I had the pleasure of being with him, did he display those characteristics of ill humor and brusqueness which have been attributed to him. It may not be gener-ally known that all his life—until he met Horace Fletcher—he suffered torments from chronic indigestion, or that it was in Fletcherism that

86

A Page from an Autograph Letter from Henry James to Horace Fletcher

he found his first relief. In a typically involved Jamesian letter to his brother William he writes (February, 1909):

It is impossible save in a long talk to make you understand how the blessed Fletcherism—so extra blessed— lulled me, charmed me, beguiled me, from the first into the convenience of not having to drag myself out into eternal walking. One must have been through what it relieved me from to know how not suffering from one's food all the while, after having suffered all one's life, and at last having it cease and vanish, could make one joyously and extravagantly relegate all out-of-door motion to a more and more casual and negligible importance. To live without the hell goad of needing to walk, with time for reading and indoor pursuits,— a delicious, insidious bribe! So, more and more, I gave up locomotion, and at last almost completely. A year and a half ago the thoracic worry began. Walking seemed to make it worse, tested by short spurts. So I thought non-walking more and more the remedy, and applied it more and more, and ate less and less, naturally. My heart was really disgusted all the while at my having ceased to call upon it. I have begun to do so again, and with the most luminous response. I am better the second half hour of my walk than the first, and better the third than the second. . . . I am, in short, returning, after an interval deplorably long and fallacious, to a due amount of reasonable exercise and a due amount of food for the same.

88

FRIENDS THROUGH TYPE

My one visit to Lamb House was in company with Horace Fletcher. The meeting with Henry James at dinner had corrected several preconceived ideas and confirmed others. Some writers are revealed by their books, others conceal themselves in their fictional prototypes. It had always been a question in my mind whether Henry James gave to his stories his own personality or received his personality from his stories. This visit settled my doubts.

The home was a perfect expression of the host, and possessed an individuality no less unique. I think it was Coventry Patmore who christened it "a jewel set in the plain,"—located as it was at the rising end of one of those meandering streets of Rye, in Sussex, England, Georgian in line and perfect in appointment.

In receiving us, Henry James gave one the impression of performing a long-established ritual. He had been reading in the garden, and when we arrived he came out into the hall with hand extended, expressing a massive cordiality.

"Welcome to my beloved Fletcher," he cried; and as he grasped my hand he said, as if by way of explanation,

"He saved my life, you know, and what is more, he improved my disposition. By rights he

89

should receive all my future royalties,—but I doubt
if he does! "

His conversation was much more intelligible
than his books. It was ponderous, but every now
and then a subtle humor relieved the impression
that he felt himself on exhibition. One could see
that he was accustomed to play the lion; but with
Fletcher present, toward whom he evidently felt
a deep obligation, he talked intimately of himself
and of the handicap his stomach infelicities had
proved in his work. The joy with which he pro⁄
claimed his emancipation showed the real man,
—a Henry James unknown to his characters or to
his public.

If William James had not taken up science as
a profession and thus become a philosopher, he
would have been a printer. No other commercial
pursuit so invited him as "the honorable, hon⁄
ored, and productive business of printing," as he
expressed it in a letter to his mother in 1863.
Naturally, with such a conception of the practice
of book manufacture, he was always particularly
concerned with the physical *format* of his volumes.
He once told me that my ability to translate his
" fool ideas " into type showed the benefit of a
Harvard education! He had no patience with

any lapse on the part of the proofreader, and when the galleys of his books reached this point in the manufacture even my most experienced readers were on the anxious seat. On the other hand, he was generous in his appreciation when a proof-reader called his attention to some slip in his copy that he had overlooked.

After his volume *Pragmatism* appeared and created such universal attention, a series of "popu-lar" lectures on the subject was announced at Cambridge. The Harpers had just published a novel of mine entitled *The Spell*, in connection with which I had devoted much time to the study of humanism and the humanists of the fifteenth century. Because of my familiarity with a kindred subject, I must confess to a sense of mortification that in reading *Pragmatism* I found myself be-yond my depth. A "popular" presentation ap-pealed to me as an opportunity for intellectual development, so I attended the first lecture, armed with pencil and notebook. Afterwards it so hap-pened that Professor James was on the trolley car when I boarded it at Harvard Square, and I sat down beside him.

"I was surprised to see you at my lecture," he remarked. "Don't you get enough of me at your office?"

I told him of my excursions into other philo-
sophic paſtures, and of my chagrin to find so little
in pragmatic fields upon which my hungry mind
could feed. He smiled at my language, and entered heartily into the spirit.

"And today?" he inquired mischievously.—
"I hope that today I guided you successfully."

"You did," I declared, opening my notebook,
and showing him the entry: "Nothing is the
only resultant of the one thing which is not."

"That led me home," I said soberly, with an
intentional double meaning.

Professor James laughed heartily.

"Did I really say that? I have no doubt I did.
It simply proves my contention that philosophers
too frequently exercise their prerogative of conceal-
ing themselves behind meaningless expressions."

Two of Professor James' typographic hobbies
were paper labels and as few words as possible on
the title page. In the matter of supplying scant
copy for the title, he won my eternal gratitude, for
many a book, otherwise typographically attraƈtive,
is ruined by overloading the title with too much
matter. This is the firſt page that catches the eye,
and its relation to the book is the same as the door
of a house. Only recently I opened a volume to
a beautiful title page. The type was perfeƈtly ar-

ranged in proportion and margin, the decoration
was charming and in complete harmony with the
type. It was set by an artist-printer and did him
credit; but turning a few more pages I found myself face to face with a red-blooded story of western
life, when the title had prepared me for something
as delicate as Milton's *L'Allegro*. A renaissance
door on a New England farmhouse would have
been equally appropriate!

I commend to those who love books the fascinating study of title pages. I entered upon it from
curiosity, and quickly found in it an abiding
hobby. The early manuscripts and first printed
volumes possessed no title pages, due probably to
the fact that the handmade paper and parchment
were so costly that the saving of a seemingly unnecessary page was a consideration. The *incipit* at
the top of the first page, reading "Here beginneth" and then adding the name of the author
and the subject, answered every purpose; and on
the last page the *explicit* marked the conclusion
of the work, and offered the printer an excellent
opportunity to record his name and the date of the
printing. Most of the early printers were modest
in recording their achievements, but in the famous
volume *De Veritate Catholicae Fidei* the printer
says of himself:

IN QUEST OF THE PERFECT BOOK

This new edition was furnished us to print in Venice by Nicolas Jenson of France. . . . Kind toward all, beneficent, generous, truthful and steadfast in the beauty, dignity, and accuracy of his printing, let me (with the indulgence of all) name him the first in the whole world; first likewise in his marvelous speed. He exists in this, our time, as a special gift from Heaven to men. June thirteen, in the year of Redemption 1489. Farewell

Bibliographers contend that the first title page was used in a book printed by Arnold Ther Hoernen of Cologne in 1470. In this volume an extra leaf is employed containing simply an introduction at the top. It has always seemed to me that this leaf is more likely to have been added by the printer to correct a careless omission of the introduction on his first page of text. Occasionally, in the humanistic manuscript volumes in the Laurenziana Library, at Florence, there occurs a "mirror" title (see *opp. page*), which consists of an illuminated page made up of a large circle in the center containing the name of the book, sometimes surrounded by smaller circles, in which are recorded the titles of the various sections. This seems far more likely to have been suggestive of what came to be the formal title page.

By the end of the fifteenth century the title page

94

Locutiones
inquinque li
brof Moyfi
·I·

Locutio
nes in
IOSVE
·II·

Contra epi
stolam parme
mam libri
Quattuor
·VIII·

Locutio
nes in libr
um iudici
·III·

Annotatio
num in
IOB
·VII·

IN HOC
VOLVMINE
CONTINENTVR
OPERA DIVI AVGV
STINI QVAE IN
CIRCVLIS SVNT
ÁDNOTÁTA·

Quefho
nef inquin
que librof
MOYSI
·IIII·

Quefho
nes in librū
Iudicum
·VI·

Quefho
nef in iesu
naue
·V·

MIRROR TITLE

From Auguftinus: *Opera Divi,* 1485.   Laurenziana Library, Florence

was in universal use, and printers showed great ingenuity in arranging the type in the form of wine cups, drinking glasses, funnels, inverted cones, and half diamonds. During the sixteenth century great artists like Dürer, Holbein, Rubens, and Mantegna executed superbly engraved titles entirely out of keeping with the poor typography of the books themselves. In many of the volumes the title page served the double purpose of title and full-page illustration (see *pages* 228 and 241). What splendid examples would have resulted if the age of engraved titles had coincided with the high-water mark in the art of printing!

As the art of printing declined, the engraved title was discarded, and the printer of the seven-teenth century seemed to feel it incumbent upon him to cover the entire page with type. If you recall the early examples of American Colonial printing, which were based upon the English models of the time, you will gain an excellent idea of the grotesque tendency of that period. The Elzevirs were the only ones who retained the engraved title (*page* 241). The Baskerville volumes (*page* 247), in the middle of the eighteenth century, showed a return to good taste and har-monious co-ordination with the text; but there was no beauty in the title until Didot in Paris and

Bodoni in Parma, Italy, introduced the so-called "modern" face, which is peculiarly well adapted to display (*page* 253). William Morris, in the late nineteenth century, successfully combined decoration with type,—over-decorated, in the minds of many, but in perfect keeping with the type pages of the volumes themselves. Cobden-Sanderson, at the Doves Press, returned to the extreme in simplicity and good taste (*page* 265), excelling all other printers in securing from the blank space on the leaf the fullest possible value. One of Cobden-Sanderson's classic remarks is, " I always give greater attention, in the typography of a book, to what I leave out than to what I put in."

The name of William Morris today may be more familiar to booklovers than that of Cobden-Sanderson, but I venture to predict that within a single decade the latter's work as printer and binder at the Doves Press at Hammersmith, London, will prove to have been a more determining factor in printing as an art than that of William Morris at the Kelmscott Press, and that the general verdict will be that Cobden-Sanderson carried out the splendid principles laid down by Morris more consistently than did that great artist-craftsman himself.

T. J. COBDEN-SANDERSON, 1841-1922
From Etching by Alphonse Legros, 1893

C-S. 1916

FRIENDS THROUGH TYPE

The story of Cobden-Sanderson's life is an interesting human document. He told it to me one evening, its significance being heightened by the simplicity of the recital. At seventeen he was apprenticed to an engineer, but he worked less than a year in the draft room. He disliked business as business, and began to read for Cambridge, with the idea of entering the Church. While at Trinity College he read for mathematical honors, but three years later, having given up all idea of going into the Church, he left Cambridge, refusing honors and a degree, which he might have had, as a protest against the competitive system and the "warp" it gave to all university teaching. Then, for seven or eight years, he devoted himself to Carlyle and the study of literature, "Chiefly German philosophy," he said, "which is perhaps not literature," supporting himself by desultory writing and practicing medicine. When he was thirty years old he was admitted to the Bar, which profession he abandoned thirteen years later to become a manual laborer. The following is quoted from notes which I made after this conversation:

I despaired of knowledge in a philosophical sense, yet I yearned to do or to make something. This was the basic idea of my life. At this time it was gradually revealed to me that the arts and crafts of life might be employed to make society itself a work of art, sound and beautiful as a whole, and in all its parts.

It is difficult to associate Cobden-Sanderson's really tremendous contributions to bookmaking as an art with his self-effacing personality. If I had met the man before I had become intimately acquainted with his work, I should have been disappointed; having had him interpreted to me by his books before I met him, his unique personality proved a definite inspiration and gave me an entirely new viewpoint on many phases of the art of typography in its application to human life.

In person, Cobden-Sanderson was of slight build, with sloping shoulders, his most noticeable feature being his reddish beard tinged with gray. He was nervous and shy, and while talking seldom looked one squarely in the eye, yet at no time could one doubt the absolute sincerity of his every word and act. He was hopelessly absentminded. Invited to dine with me in London, he appeared the evening before the date set, retiring overwhelmed with embarrassment when he discovered his mistake. On the following evening he forgot the appointment altogether! Later, when in Boston, he accepted an invitation to dine with a literary society, but failed to appear because he could not remember where the dinner was to be held. He had mislaid his note of invitation and could not recall the name of the man who sent it. On that evening he dashed madly around the city in a taxicab for over an hour, finally ending up at his hotel in absolute exhaustion while the members of the literary society dined without their lion!

While president of the Society of Printers in Boston, I arranged for Cobden-Sanderson to come to America to deliver some lectures on *The Ideal Book.* Among these were four given at Harvard University. At the conclusion of the last lecture he came to my library, thoroughly tired out and completely discouraged. Seated in a great easy chair he remained for several moments in absolute silence, resting his face upon his hands. Suddenly, without a moment's warning, he straightened up and said with all the vehemence at his command,

" I am the veriest impostor who ever came to your shores! "

Seeing my surprise and incredulity, he added,

" I have come to America to tell you people how to make books. In New York they took me to see the great Morgan Library and other collections. They showed me rare *incunabula.* They expected me to know all about them, and to be enthusiastic over them. As a matter of fact, I know nothing about the work of the great master-printers, and care less!"

My face must have disclosed my thoughts, for he held up a restraining hand.

"Don't think me such an egotist as my words imply. It isn't that at all. It is true that I am interested only in my own work, but that is because my work means something more to me than the books I produce. When I print a book or bind one it is because I have a message in my soul which I am impelled to give mankind, and it comes out through my fingers. Other men express their messages in different *media,*—in stone or on canvas. I have discovered that the book is my medium. When I bind and decorate a volume I seem to be setting myself, like a magnetized needle, or like an ancient temple, in line and all square, not alone with my own ideal of society, but with that orderly and rhythmical whole which is the revelation of science and the normal of developed humanity. You asked me a while ago to explain certain inconsistencies in my work, and I told you that there was no explanation. That is because each piece of work represents me at the time I do it. Sometimes it is good and sometimes poor, but, in any case, it stands as the expression of myself at the time I did it."

FRIENDS THROUGH TYPE

As he spoke I wondered if Cobden-Sanderson had not explained why, in the various arts, the work of those master-spirits of the past had not been surpassed or even equaled during the intervening centuries. It is a matter for consideration, when the world has shown such spectacular advance along material lines, that in painting, in sculpture, in architecture, in printing, the work of the old masters still stands supreme. In their time, when men had messages in their souls to give the world, the interpretation came out through their fingers, expressed in the medium with which each was familiar. Before the invention of printing, the masses received those messages directly from the marble or the canvas, or from the design of some great building. The printed book opened to the world a storehouse of wisdom hitherto unavailable, and made individual effort less conspicuous and therefore less demanded. The few outstanding figures in every art have been those who, like Cobden-Sanderson, have set themselves "in line and all square, not alone with their own ideals of society, but with that orderly and rhythmical whole which is the revelation of science and the normal of developed humanity." It is what Cobden-Sanderson has done rather than his written words, that conveys the greatest message.

IN QUEST OF THE PERFECT BOOK

While Theodore Roosevelt was President of the United States, and on the occasion of one of his several visits to Boston, his secretary wrote that the President would like to examine with me some of the special volumes I had built. I knew him to be an omnivorous reader, but until then did not realize his deep interest in the physical side of books.

He came to the University Press one bitterly cold day in January, and entered my office wrapped in a huge fur coat. After greeting him I asked if he wouldn't lay the coat aside.

"Of course I will," he replied briskly; "it is just as easy to catch hot as it is to catch cold."

We devoted ourselves for an hour to an examination and discussion of certain volumes I had produced. One of these was a small twelve-mo entitled *Trophies of Heredia,* containing poems by a Spanish poet which had been brought out in artistic *format* for a Boston publishing house, but had proved a complete failure from a commercial standpoint. Probably not over two hundred copies of the book were ever sold. Evidently one of these had fallen into the President's hands, for he seized my copy eagerly, saying,

"Hello! I didn't remember that you made this. Extraordinary volume, isn't it? I want to show you something."

Quickly turning to one of the pages he pointed to the line, *The hidden warmth of the Polar Sea.*

" What do you think of that? " he demanded. " Did you ever think of the Polar Sea as being warm? And by Jove he's right,—it *is* warm! "

Later, in Washington, I accepted his invitation for luncheon at the White House and for an afternoon in his library, where we continued our discussion of books. Before we turned to the volumes, he showed me some of the unusual presents which various potentates had given him, such as a jade bear from the Tzar of Russia, a revolver from Admiral Togo, and line drawings made personally by the Kaiser, showing in detail every ship in our Navy. When I expressed surprise that such exact knowledge should be in the possession of another country, my host became serious.

" The Kaiser is a most extraordinary fellow," he said deliberately,—" not every one realizes how extraordinary. He and I have corresponded ever since I became President, and I tell you that if his letters were ever published they would bring on a world war. Thank God I don't have to leave them behind when I retire. That's one prerogative the President has, at any rate."

I often thought of these comments after the World War broke out. An echo of them came while the desperate struggle was in full force. Ernest Harold Baynes, nature-lover and expert on birds, was visiting at my house, having dined with the ex-President at Oyster Bay the week before. In speaking of the dinner, Baynes said that Roosevelt declared that had he been President, Germany would never have forced the war at the time she did. When pressed to explain, Roosevelt said:

" The Kaiser would have remembered what he outlined to me in some letters he wrote while I was President. Bill knows me, and I know Bill! "

From the library we extended our examination to the family living-room, where there were other volumes of interest on the tables or in the book-cases. From these, the President picked up a hand-lettered, illuminated manuscript which he had just received as a present from King Menelik of Abyssinia. Some one had told him that it was a manuscript of the twelfth or thirteenth century, but to a student of the art of illumination it was clearly a modern copy of an old manuscript. The hand lettering was excellent, but the decoration included colors impossible to secure with the ancient pigments, and the parchment was distinctly of modern origin.

" You are just the one to tell me about this," Mr. Roosevelt exclaimed. " Is it an original manuscript? "

He so obviously wished to receive an affirmative reply that I temporized by asking if some letter of description had not come with it.

" Oh, yes," he replied, immediately divining the occasion of my question and showing his disappointment; " there was a missive, which is now in the archives of the State Department. I saw a translation of it, but it is only one of those banal expressions similar to any one of my own utterances, when I cable, for instance, to my imperial brother, the Emperor of Austria, how touched and moved I am to learn that his cousin, the lady with the ten names, has been safely delivered of a child! "

The President was particularly interested in the subject of illustration, and he showed me several examples, asking for a description of the various processes. From that we passed on to a discussion of the varying demand from the time when I first began to make books. I explained that the development of the halftone plate and of the four-color process plates had been practically within this period,—that prior to 1890 the excessive cost of woodcuts, steel engravings, or lithography confined illustration to expensive volumes. The halftone opened the way for profuse illustration at minimum expense.

The President showed me an impression from one of Timothy Cole's marvelous woodcuts, and we agreed that the halftone had never taken the place of any process that depends upon the hand for execution. The very perfection to which the art of halftone reproduction has been carried is a danger point in considering the permanence of its popularity. This does not apply to its use in news-papers, but in reproducing with such slavish fidel-ity photographs of objects perpetuated in books of permanent value. It seemed paradoxical to say that the nearer perfection an art attains the less interesting it becomes, because the very variation incidental to hand work in any art is what relieves the monotony of that perfection attained through mechanical means. Since then, a few leading en-gravers have demonstrated how the halftone may be improved by hand work. This combination has opened up new possibilities that guarantee its continued popularity.

With the tremendous increase in the cost of manufacturing books during and since the World War, publishers found that by omitting illustra-tions from their volumes they could come nearer

to keeping the cost within the required limits, so
for a period illustrated volumes became
limited in number

There is no question that the public loves pictures,
and the development during recent years of so-
called newspapers from which the public gleans
the daily news by means of halftone illustrations,
is, in a way, a reversion to the time before the
printing press, when the masses received their
education wholly through pictorial design. The
popularity of moving pictures is another evidence.
I have always wished that this phase had developed at the time of our discussion, for I am sure
Mr. Roosevelt would have had some interesting
comments to make on its significance. I like to
believe that this tendency will correct itself, for,
after all, the pictures which are most worth
while are those which we ourselves draw
subconsciously from impressions made
through intellectual
exploits

CHAPTER IV
The Lure of Illumination

IV
THE LURE OF ILLUMINATION

SITTING one day in the librarian's office in the Laurenziana Library, in Florence, the conversation turned upon the subject of illumination. Taking a key from his pocket, my friend Guido Biagi unlocked one of the drawers in the ancient wooden desk in front of him, and lifted from it a small, purple vellum case, inlaid with jewels. Opening it carefully, he exposed a volume similarly bound and similarly adorned. Then, as he turned the leaves, and the full splendor of the masterpiece was spread out before me,—the marvelous delicacy of design, the gorgeousness of color, the magnificence of decoration and miniature,—I drew in my breath excitedly, and bent nearer to the magnifying glass which was required in tracing the intricacy of the work.

This was a *Book of Hours* illuminated by Francesco d'Antonio del Cherico, which had once belonged to Lorenzo de' Medici, and was representative of the best of the fifteenth-century Italian work (*page* 146). The hand letters were

written by Antonio Sinibaldi in humanistic characters upon the finest and rarest parchment; the
illumination, with its beaten gold and gorgeous
colors, was so close a representation of the jewels
themselves as to make one almost believe that the
gems were inlaid upon the page! And it was the
very volume that had many times rested in the
hands of Lorenzo the Magnificent, as it was at
that moment resting in mine!

For the first time the art of illumination became
real to me,—not something merely to be gazed at
with respect and admiration, but an expression of
artistic accomplishment to be studied and understood, and made a part of one's life.

The underlying thought that has inspired illumination in books from its very beginning is
more interesting even than the splendid pages
which challenge one's comprehension and almost
pass beyond his power of understanding. To the
ancients, as we have seen, the rarest gems in all the
world were gems of thought. The book was the
tangible and visible expression of man's intellect,
worthy of the noblest presentation. These true
lovers of books engaged scribes to write the text in
minium of rare brilliancy brought from India or
Spain, or in Byzantine ink of pure Oriental gold;
they selected, to write upon, the finest material

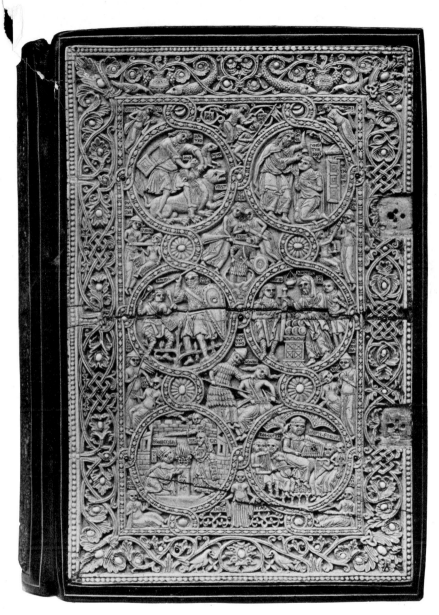

CARVED IVORY BINDING
Jeweled with Rubies and Turquoises
From *Psalter* (12th Century). Brit. Mus. Eger. MS. 1139
(Reduced in size)

possible,—sometimes nothing less than virgin parchment, soft as velvet, made from the skins of still-born kids; they employed the greatest artists of the day to draw decorations or to paint miniatures; and they enclosed this glorified thought of man, now perpetuated for all time, in a cover devised sometimes of tablets of beaten gold, or of ivory inlaid with precious jewels (*page* 112).

For centuries, this glorification was primarily bestowed upon religious manuscripts, and illumination came to be associated with the Church, but by the fourteenth century the art ceased to be confined to the cloister. Wealthy patrons recognized that it offered too splendid a medium of expression to permit limitation; and lay artists were employed to add their talents in increasing the illuminated treasures of the world.

There would seem to be no reason why so satisfying an art as that of illumination should not continue to be employed to make beautifully printed books still more beautiful, yet even among those who really love and know books there is a surprising lack of knowledge concerning this fascinating work. The art of Raphael and Rubens has been a part of our everyday life and is familiar to us; but the names of Francesco d'Antonio, Jean Foucquet, and Jean Bourdichon have never become household words, and the masterpieces of the illuminator's art which stand to their credit seem almost shrouded in a hazy and mysterious indefiniteness.

I have learned from my own experience that even fragmentary study brings rich rewards:—the interest in discovering that instead of being merely decorative, the art of illumination is as definitive in recording the temporary or fashionable customs of various periods as history itself. There is a satisfaction in learning to distinguish the characteristics of each well-defined school:—of recognizing the fretted arcades and mosaics of church decoration in the Romanesque style; the stained glass of the Gothic cathedrals in the schools of England, France, Germany, or Italy; the love of flower cultivation in the work of the Netherlandish artists; the echo of the skill of the goldsmith and enameller in the French manuscripts; and the glory of the gem cutter in those of the Italian Renaissance. There is the romance connected with each great masterpiece as it passes from artist to patron, and then on down the centuries, commemorating loyal devotion to saintly attributes; expressing fealty at coronations or congratulations at Royal marriages; conveying expressions of devotion and affection from noble lords and ladies, one to the other. Illuminated volumes were not the playthings of the common people, and in their peregrinations to their final resting places in libraries and museums, they passed along a Royal road and became clothed with fascinating associations.

There was a time when I thought I knew enough about the various schools to recognize the locality of origin or the approximate date of a manuscript, but I soon learned my presumption. Illuminators of one country, particularly of France, scattered themselves all over Europe, retaining the basic principles of their own national style, yet adding to it something significant of the country in which they worked. Of course, there are certain external evidences which help. The vellum itself tells a story: if it is peculiarly white and fine, and highly polished, the presumption is that it is Italian or dates earlier than the tenth century; if very thin and soft, it was made from the skins of still-born calves or kids, and is probably of the thirteenth or fourteenth centuries.

The colors, too, contribute their share. Each old-time artist ground or mixed his own pigments, —red and blue, and less commonly yellow, green, purple, black, and white. Certain shades are characteristic of certain periods. The application of gold differs from time to time: in England, for instance, gold powder was used until the twelfth century, after which date gold leaf is beautifully laid on the sheet. The raised-gold letters and decorations were made by building up with a peculiar clay, after the design had been drawn in outline, over which the gold leaf was skilfully laid and burnished with an agate.

As the student applies himself to the subject, one clue leads him to another, and he pursues his search with a fascination that soon becomes an obsession. That chance acquaintance with Francesco d'Antonio inspired me to become better acquainted with this art. It took me into different monasteries and libraries, always following "the quest," and lured me on to further seeking by learning of new beauties for which to search, and of new examples to be studied. Even as I write this, I am told that at Chantilly, in the Musée Condé, the *Très Riches Heures* of the Duc de Berry is the most beautiful example of the French school. I have never seen it, and I now have a new objective on my next visit to France!

In this quest, covering many years, I have come to single out certain manuscripts as signifying to me certain interesting developments in the art during its evolution, and I study them whenever the opportunity offers. It is of these that I make a record here. Some might select other examples as better illustrative from their own viewpoints; some might draw conclusions different from mine from the same examples,—and we might all be right!

There is little for us to examine in our pilgrimage until the Emperor Justinian, after the conflagration in the year 532, which completely wiped out Constantinople with its magnificent monuments, reconstructed and rebuilt the city. There are two copies of *Virgil* at the Vatican Library in Rome, to be sure, which are earlier than that, and form links in the chain between illumination as illustration and as book decoration; there is the *Roman Calendar* in the Imperial Library at Vienna, in which for the first time is combined decoration with illustration; there is the *Ambrosiana Homer* at Milan, of which an excellent reproduction may be found in any large library,—made under the supervision of Achille Ratti, before he became Pope Pius XI; there are the burnt fragments of the *Cottonian Genesis* at the British Museum in London,—none more than four inches square, and running down to one inch, some perforated with holes, and almost obliterated, others still preserving the ancient colors of the design, with the Greek letters clearly legible after sixteen centuries.

These are historical and interesting, but we are seeking beauty. In the splendor of the rebirth of Constantinople, to which all the known world contributed gold, and silver, and jewels, medieval illumination found its beginning. Artists could now afford to send to the Far East and to the southern shores of Europe for their costly materials. Brilliant *minium* came from India and from Spain, *lapis lazuli* from Persia and Bokhara, and the famous Byzantine gold ink was manufactured by the illuminators themselves out of pure Oriental gold. The vellum was stained with rose and scarlet tints and purple dyes, upon which the gold and silver inks contrasted with marvelous brilliancy.

Gorgeousness was the fashion of the times in everything from architecture to dress, and in the wealth and sumptuous materials at their command the artists mistook splendor for beauty. The Byzantine figure work is based upon models as rigid as those of the Egyptians, and shows little life or variety (*opp. page*). Landscapes and trees are symbolic and fanciful. Buildings have no regard for relative proportions, and are tinted merely as parts of the general color scheme. The illumi-

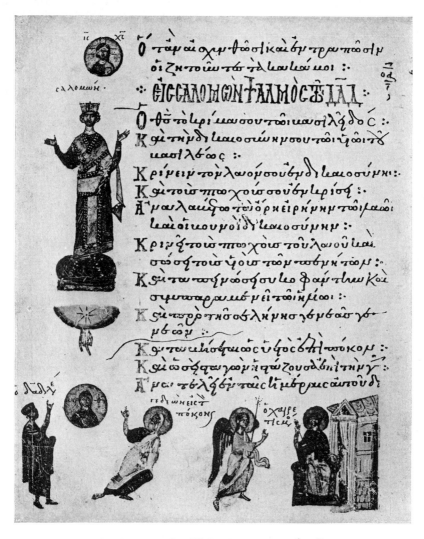

PSALTER IN GREEK. *Byzantine,* 11th Century
Solomon, David, Gideon, and the Annunciation
(Brit. Mus. Add. MS. 19352.   9¼ x 8 inches)

nators adhered so closely to mechanical rules that the volumes lack even individuality.

There are comparatively few of these extravagant relics now in existence. Their intrinsic value made them favorite objects of pillage, and hundreds were destroyed for their jewels and precious metals. In many of those that have endured, like the *Codex Argenteus,* at Upsala, in Sweden, the silver letters have turned black, the gold ink has become a rusty red, and the stained vellum now supplies a tawdry background.

After passing the early stages of the art, there are ten examples I particularly like to keep fresh in my mind as showing the evolution of that insatiable desire on the part of booklovers of all ages to enrich the book. Four of these are in the British Museum in London, four in the Bibliothèque Nationale in Paris, one in the Library of San Marco in Venice, and one in the Laurenziana Library in Florence. In each of these storehouses of treasure there are many other manuscripts worthy of all the time a pilgrim can spare; but these ten represent different schools and different epochs, and in my own study have combined to make illumination a living art and a romantic history.

The *Lindisfarne Gospels* is where I start my

illuminated pilgrimage. It takes me back to the seventh century, when the world was shrouded in darkest ignorance, and is a reminder that except for the development in the Irish monasteries, as typified by early illuminated volumes such as this, knowledge of books might have almost wholly disappeared. It recalls the asceticism of those early Irish monks carried even to a point of fanaticism; their toilsome pilgrimages to Rome, visiting the different monasteries and collecting, one by one, the manuscripts to bring back to form those early libraries that kept alive the light of learning.

The Irish school of writing and painting passed over to England through the monasteries established by the Irish monks in Scotland, and the earliest of the English settlements was Lindisfarne. It was here that the *Gospels,* one of the most characteristic examples of the Celtic School, as translated to northern England, was produced. Such knowledge of its date and origin as exists rests upon a colophon added at the end of the manuscript, probably in the tenth century, which would seem to place the date of the execution of the work at about the year 700. For nearly two centuries it remained as the chief treasure of Lindisfarne. In 875, so the tradition runs, in order to escape from the invasion of the Danes, it was decided to remove the body of Saint Cuthbert and the most valued relics to the mainland, and the *Gospels* was included. When the attempt was made to cross over to Ireland, according to the legend, the ship was driven back by storm, and the chest containing the precious volume was lost overboard. Here is the quaint chronicle:

In this storm, while the ship was lying over on her side, a copy of the Gospels, adorned with gold and precious stones, fell overboard and sank into the depths of the sea. Accordingly, after a little while, they bend their knees and prostrate themselves at full length before the feet of the sacred body, asking pardon for their foolish venture. Then they seize the helm and turn the ship back to the shore and to their fellows, and immediately they arrive there without any difficulty, the wind blowing astern . . . Amidst their lamentations in this distress, at length the accustomed help of their pious patron came to their aid, whereby their minds were relieved from grief and their bodies from labor, seeing that the Lord is a refuge of the poor, a helper in time of trouble. For, appearing in a vision to one of them, Hunred by name, he bade them seek, when the tide was low, for the manuscript . . .; for, perchance, beyond the utmost they could hope, they would, by the mercy of God, find it. . . . Accordingly they go to the sea and find that it had retired much farther than it was accustomed; and after walking three miles or more they find the sacred manuscript of the Gospels *itself, exhibiting all its outer splendor of jewels and gold and all the beauty of its pages and writing within, as though it had never been touched by water. . . . And this is believed to be due to the merits of Saint Cuthbert himself and of those who made the book, namely Bishop Eadfrith of holy memory, who wrote it with his own hand in honor of the blessed Cuthbert; and the venerable Æthelwald, his successor, who caused it to be adorned with gold and precious stones; and Saint Billfrith the anchorite, who, obeying with skilled hands the wishes of his superior, achieved an excellent work. For he excelled in the goldsmith's art.*

This quotation from Mr. Eric George Millar's Introduction to the facsimile reproduction of this famous manuscript, published by the British Museum, is given at such length to emphasize at the very beginning of this pilgrimage the important place given to these manuscripts in the communities for which they were prepared. The fact that such a legend exists at all attests the personality the manuscript had assumed. It was my very great pleasure, the last time I studied the *Gospels*, to have Mr. Millar, who is an Assistant in the Department of Manuscripts at the British Museum, explain many things in connection with it which could not be gleaned without the exhaustive study which he has given to it.

THE LURE OF ILLUMINATION

The *Gospels* includes 258 leaves of heavy vellum, measuring about 13 by 10 inches. The Latin text is written in beautifully designed, *semi-uncial* characters. These differ from the capital letters only by their relatively greater roundness, inclination, and inequality in height. This style of lettering obtained until the eighth or ninth century, when the semi-uncial character became the transition to the minuscule. There are five full pages of decoration, in cruciform design of most extraordinary elaboration; six pages of ornamented text; four full-page miniatures of the Evangelists, in which the scribes are drawn in profile, seated, with cushion, desk, and footstool; sixteen pages of Canon tables, decorated in pure Celtic style; and numerous initials of various sizes.

The great interest in this manuscript lies in the cruciform pages. When I first saw them I thought the work a marvelous example of the amount of intricate design an artist could devise within a given area of space. Then, as I studied them, came the realization that, complicated as they were, there was a definite plan the artist had established and followed which preserved the balance of coloring and design.

In the illustration here given (*page* 124), Mr. Millar showed me how he has ingeniously unraveled the knots. It is peculiarly interesting as it demonstrates the methods by which the expert is able to understand much that the casual observer fails to see. He pointed out that the background of the page is occupied by a design of no less than 88 birds, arranged in a perfect pattern, with 7 at the top, 7 at the bottom, 9 on each side, 12 in the gaps between the outer panels, four groups of 10 surrounding the rectangular panels, and 4 single birds in the gaps between the points of the cross and the T panels. The necks and the bodies are so cleverly balanced that even when at first the scheme seems inconsistent, further examination shows that the artist adhered religiously to his plan. The color arrangement is carried out with equal thought and care.

The four miniatures of the Evangelists show Byzantine influence, but in the features, and the hair, and in the frames, the Celtic style prevails. Gold is used only on two pages.

The *Lindisfarne Gospels* cannot be called beautiful when compared with the work of later centuries, but can we fully appreciate the beauty we are approaching without becoming familiar, step by step, with what led up to it? In this manuscript the precious Gospels were enriched by the labor of devoted enthusiasts in the manner they knew

THE LINDISFARNE GOSPELS. *Celtic,* about A.D. 700
(Brit. Mus. Cotton MS. Nero. D. iv. $12\frac{1}{2}$ x 10 inches)

beft, and with an ingenuity and induftry that ftaggers us today. Taking what the paft had taught them, they gave to it their own interpretation, and thus advanced the art toward its final consummation and glory.

Taken merely as an example of illumination, few would share my interest in the *Alcuin Bible*, a Carolingian manuscript of the ninth century; but to any one interested in printing, this huge volume at the British Museum cannot be overlooked. In the eighth century the Irish and AngloSaxon missionary artifts transplanted their work to their settlements on the Continent, out of which sprang the Carolingian School in France,—so named in honor of Charlemagne. Sacred compositions, derived largely from Latin and Byzantine sources, were now added to the highly ornamental letters. Solid backgrounds were abandoned, and handsome architectural designs were used to frame the miniatures.

If you will examine the *Alcuin Bible* with me, you will note what a tremendous advance has been made. The manuscript is a copy of the Vulgate said to be revised and amended by Alcuin of York to present to Charlemagne on the occasion of that monarch's coronation. Some dispute this tradition altogether; some claim that a similar Bible, now in Rome, is entitled to the honor; but the controversy does not detract from the interest in the book itself. This Alcuin of York was the instrument of Charlemagne in establishing the reform in hand lettering, which has been of the utmost importance in the history of printing. Starting with the foundation of the School of Tours in 796, the *minuscule*, or lower-case letter, which is the basis of our modern styles, superceded all other forms of hand lettering. By the twelfth century the clear, free-flowing form that developed from the Caroline minuscule was the most beautiful hand ever developed, and was never surpassed until the humanistic scribes of the fifteenth century took it in its Italian form as their model and perfected it.

The volume is a large quarto, 20 by 14½ inches in size, splendidly written in double column in minuscule characters with uncial initials (*opp. page*). There are four full-page illuminations, and many smaller miniatures, with characteristic architectural detail that show Roman influence, while the decorations themselves are reminiscent of the Byzantine and the Celtic Schools.

It is the hand lettering rather than the illumina tion or the decoration that particularly interests

126

eiret afacietua inimicum · Diceteq: contere
rete · habitabit isrt confidenter ecsolus· Oculi
iacob interra frumenta etuini · caeliq: caliga
bunt rore · Beatus esauisrt quis similis tui
populequisaluaris· Indno scutum auxiliatui
etgladius gloriaetuae· negabunce inimica
tui etueorum colla calcabis Ascendit ergo *Cap:34*
morses decam pecerib: moab supermontem
nebo inueracem falga contrahericho
ostenditq: et dns omnem terram galaad usq:
dan · etuniuersum nepthali terramq: ephra
im etmanasse etomne terram usq: admaye
nouissimu · etaustralem partem · etlatitu
dinem campi hiericho ciuitatis palmarum
usq: segor· Dixitq: dns adeum · Haec éterra
proquaiuraui abraam isaac etiacob dicens·
seminituo daboeam · Uidisti eam oculistuis
etnontransibis adillam ·

M
ortuusqi é ibi morses seruus dni interra
moab iubentedno · etsepeliuit eum inualle
terrae moab contra phogor· etnoncognouit
homo sepulchrum eius usq: inpresentem diem ·
Morses centum etuiginti annorum erat quan
domortuusé noncaligauit oculus eius· nec
dentes illius motisunt · Fleueruntq: eum fili
israhel incampecerib: moab triginta dieb: et
completasdies planctus lugentium morsen Iosue uero
filius nun repletus é spusapientiae quia mor
ses posuit super eu manus suas · etoboedierunt
ei fili isrl · feceruntq: sicut precepit
dns morsi ·

E
tnonsurrexit propheta ultra insisrl sicut
morses quem nossetdns facie adfaciem ·
Inomnib: signis atq: portentis quae misit
pereum ut faceret interra aegypti pha
raoni etomnib: seruis eius uniuersaeque
terrae illius etcunctam manum robustam
magnaq: mirabilia quae fecit morses
coram uniuerso israhel ·

EXPLICIT ADDABARIM

QVOD GRECE DICITUR

DEUTERONOMIVM

HABET VERS· II DC

T
ANDEMFINITOPEN
tatheuco moysi uidut grandi fae
nore liberati adiesum filium naue
manu mitamus· quem hebraei iosue
bennun id· éiosue filium nun uocant
et adiudicu librum quem sopthim
appellant· Adruth quoq: et hester quos isde
nominib: efferunt· monemusq: lectorem
ut siluam ebraicoru nominum etdisinctio
nes per membra diuisas diligens scriptor
conseruet· neé noster labor etillius stu
dium pereat· Etutin primis quodsae
petetatus sum sciat me non inreprehen
sione ueterum noua cudere sicut amiui mea
criminantur· sed prouiribus partem offerre
linguae meae hominib: quostamen nra
delectant utprograecoru· EΞΑΠΛΟΙC
quae éésumptu etlabore maximo indigent·
editionem nrram habeant· Etsicubinan
tiquoru uoluminum lectione dubitarint
haec illis conferentes inueniant quod re
quirunt· Maxime cum apudlatinos tot
sint exemplaria quot codices· Etunusquisq:
proarbitriosuo uel addiderit uel subtraxerit
quodei uisum· é· Etutiq: nonpossit uerum ee
quoddisisonat· Unde ceese arcuato uulne
recontra nos insurgere scorpius et sem
opus uenenata carpere linguad desisat
uel suscipiens siplacet uel contempnens
sidisplicet· Meminerit q: illorum uer suu
ósuum abundauit nequitia etlingua
tua concinnabat dolos· sedens aduersus
fratrem tuum loquebaris· etaduersus
filiu matristuae ponebas scandalum
haec fecisti étacui· Existimasti inique
quod erotui similis· arguam te ésataua
contra faciem tuam· Quae enim audi
enas utilitatis· é nos laborando sudare·

me. When I first began my work in designing my Humanistic type, I was amazed that the humanistic scribes of the fifteenth century, upon whose letters I based my own, could have so suddenly taken such a stride forward. The mere fact that there was a greater demand for their work did not seem to explain the phenomenon. Then I discovered that these fifteenth-century artists, instead of adapting or copying the Caroline minuscule, set about to perfect it. They mastered the principles upon which it was based, and with the technical advantages that had come to them through the intervening centuries, brought the design to its fullest beauty.

To supplement my study of the *Alcuin Bible,* I turn to the masterpiece of the Carolingian School in the Bibliothèque Nationale in Paris. *The Golden Gospels of Saint Médard* belongs to the same period as the *Alcuin Bible,* and its hand letters are of the same beautiful design, but more brilliant in that they are written throughout in gold. In spite of the crude and unnatural figures, I am always impressed with a feeling that the artist is, for the first time, making a definite effort to break away from past tradition toward more natural design. The Byzantine atmosphere still clings to the work as a whole (*page* 128), but in the frames and the backgrounds there is an echo of the ivory carving and the architecture of the new Church of San Vitale at Ravenna, and the power-ful influence of the early Christian symbolism asserts itself in the miniatures.

The hand-lettered pages are enclosed in plain borders of green or red tint, with outside rules of gold. Each picture page covers the entire leaf. Every now and then, superimposed upon the solid background of the margins, are tiny figures so far superior in freedom of design to the major subjects as to make one wonder why the more pretentious efforts are not farther advanced than they are. Yet why should we be surprised that an artist, under the influence of centuries of precedent and the ever-present aversion to change, should move slowly in expressing originality? As it is, the pages of *Saint Médard* give us for the first time motivation for the glorious development of the art to come in the fourteenth and fifteenth centuries.

The rise of Gothic influence forms the great dividing line between the old, or ecclesiastic, and the new, or naturalistic, spirit in monastic art. The *Psalter of Saint Louis*, a Gothic manuscript

GOLDEN GOSPELS OF ST. MÉDARD. *Carolingian,* 9th Century
(Bibl. Nat. MS. Lat. 8850. 12 x 7½ inches)

of the thirteenth century, in the Bibliothèque Nationale in Paris, is an example of this transition that I like to study.

By the beginning of the thirteenth century the initial—which in the Celtic style had dominated the entire page—was losing its supremacy, becoming simply one factor in the general scheme. A delicate fringe work or filigree of pen flourishes, which had sprung up around the initial as it became reduced in size, was later to be converted into a tendril or cylindrical stem, bearing a succession of five leaves and leaflets of ivy, usually entirely filled with burnished gold. Small figures, and, later, groups of figures, take the place of the linear ornament in the interior of the letter, and calligraphy and miniature painting become successfully fused. An exact date cannot be assigned, as it was the result of a slow and gradual growth.

From certain references made in the Calendar pages of the *Psalter*, it is evident that the manuscript was copied and illuminated between the year 1252, when Queen Blanche of Castile died, and the death of Saint Louis in 1270. What a story this book could tell! Written in French in red ink on one of the front end leaves is this inscription:

This Psalter of Saint Louis was given by Queen Jeanne d'Evreux to King Charles, son of King John, in the year

129

of our Master, 1369; and the present King Charles, son of the said King Charles, gave it to Madame Marie of France, his daughter, a nun at Poissy, on Saint Michel's Day, in the year 1400

The *Psalter* contains 260 leaves of parchment, 8½ by 6 inches. Of these, seventy-eight are small, beautiful miniatures, depicting the principal scenes in the early books of the Old Testament, and eight are illustrations to the Psalms (*page* 132), the remaining leaves being occupied by the text. In these miniatures is shown a refinement and delicacy of treatment combined with unusual freedom in execution. Here is one of the best examples of the reflection of the stained-glass windows of the Gothic cathedrals (*opp. page*), to which reference has already been made. There is no shading whatever. The body color is laid on the design in flat tints, finished by strokes of the pen.

All this is interesting because this period marks the end of the needless limitations illuminators placed upon themselves. Working on vellum as a medium instead of in glass with lead outlines, should be a much simpler operation! Still, one can't help reveling in the bright scarlet and the rich blue of the stained glass, and would be loath to give it up.

PSALTER OF SAINT LOUIS. *Gothic,* 13th Century
Abraham and Isaac
(Bibl. Nat. MS. Lat. 10525. 8½ x 6 inches)

THE LURE OF ILLUMINATION

The volume is bound in old boards, covered with blue and rose material embossed with silver and reinforced with velvet. The clasps are gone.

The style of illumination in the thirteenth century shows no distinct national characteristics, for, even in England, some of the work was executed by French artists. The initial is usually set within a frame shaped to its outline, the ground being either of gold, slightly raised or burnished, or of color, especially dark blue and pale tints of salmon, gray, or violet, sometimes edged with gold.

Queen Mary's Psalter, a superb example of the English School in the early fourteenth century, is a landmark in our pilgrimage because, in addition to its surpassing beauty, it is an example of illumination sought for its own artistic value instead of being associated wholly with devotional manuscripts. No one can examine the charming series of little tinted drawings in the margins of the Litany without being convinced that the artist, whoever he may have been, was quite familiar with the world outside the Church (see *frontispiece*).

The earliest note of ownership in this manuscript is of the sixteenth century:

This boke was sume tyme the Erle of Rutelands, and it was his wil that it shulde by successioun all way go to the

*lande of Ruteland or to him that linyally suceedes by reson
of inheritaunce in the saide lande.*

How fascinating these records are, made by
different hands as the precious manuscripts are
passed on down the ages! Even though we have
no absolute knowledge of which Rutland is meant,
an added personality is given to the pages we are
now permitted to turn and to admire. In this
manuscript there is also a second note, written in
Latin on the fly leaf at the end, paying a tribute
to a certain Baldwin Smith, "an honest customs
officer," who frustrated an attempt to ship the
volume out of England, and presented it to Queen
Mary. It is now in the British Museum.

Whether or not this was Queen Mary's first
acquaintance with the manuscript is not known,
but from the binding she put on it she surely considered it a highly prized personal possession. It
would naturally be of special interest to her because of its connection with the old liturgy she was
so anxious to restore. The silver-gilt clasp fittings
are missing now. The crimson velvet with the
pomegranate, the Queen's badge, worked in
colored silks and gold thread on each cover, are
worn and shabby; but on the corner plates the
engraved lion, dragon, portcullis, and fleur-de-lys
of the Tudors are still triumphant.

Jncensa igni et suffossa: ab incrpatione
uultus tui peribunt.
Fiat manus tua super uirum dextere tue:
τ sup filium hominis quē confirmasti t.
Et non discedimus a te: uiuificabis nos τ
nomen tuum inuocabimus.
Domine deus uirtutum conuerte nos: et
ostende faciem tuam τ salui erimus.

PSALTER OF SAINT LOUIS. *Gothic*, 13th Century
Psalms lxviii. 1-3
(Bibl. Nat. MS. Lat. 10525. 8½ x 6 inches)

THE LURE OF ILLUMINATION

The manuscript, executed upon thin vellum, and consisting of 320 leaves about 11 by 7 inches, opens with a series of 228 pen and ink drawings. In most cases there are two designs on each page, illustrating Bible history from the Creation down to the death of Solomon (*page* 134). With the drawings is a running description in French, sometimes in prose, sometimes in rhyme, which in itself is interesting, as the story does not always confine itself strictly to the Biblical records but occasionally embodies apocryphal details.

The drawings themselves are exquisite, and in the skill of execution mark another tremendous advance in the art of illumination. They are delicately tinted with violet, green, red, and brown. The frame is a plain band of vermilion, from each corner of which is extended a stem with three leaves tinted with green or violet.

Following the series of drawings comes a full page showing the Tree of Jesse, and three other full pages depicting the Saints, — one page of four compartments and two of six. The text, from this point, represents the usual form of the liturgical Psalter, the Psalms being preceded by a Calendar, two pages to a month, and followed by the Canticles, including the Athanasian Creed, and then by the Litany. In the Psalter, the miniatures show

133

incidents from the life of Christ; the Canticles depict scenes from the Passion; while in the Litany are miniatures of the Saints and Martyrs. The initials themselves are elaborate, many containing small miniatures, and all lighted up with brilliant colors and burnished gold. In the Litany, in addition to the religious subjects, there are splendid little scenes of every-day life painted in the lower margins which make the manuscript unique,— illustrations of the Bestiary, tilting and hunting scenes, sports and pastimes, grotesque figures and combats, dancers and musicians. The manuscript ends with the Miracles of the Virgin and the Lives and Passions of the Saints.

In *Queen Mary's Psalter,* and in manuscripts from this period to those of the sixteenth century, we find ourselves reveling in sheer beauty. "Why not have started here?" asks my reader. Perhaps we should have done so; but this is a record not of what I ought to do, but of what I've done! To see one beautiful manuscript after another, without being able to recognize what makes each one different and significant, would take away my pleasure, for the riotous colors and gold would merge one into another. Is it not true that there comes greater enjoyment in better understanding? We admire what we may not understand, but

QUEEN MARY'S PSALTER. *English,* 14th Century
From the Life of Joseph
(Brit. Mus. Royal MS. 2B vii. 11 x 7 inches)

without underſtanding there can be no complete appreciation. In this case, familiarity breeds content!

After ſtudying the beſt of fourteenth-century English illumination in _Queen Mary's Psalter_, I like to turn to the _Bedford Book of Hours_, to make comparison with one of the most beautiful French manuscripts of a century later. This is also at the British Museum, so in the brief space of time required by the attendant to change the volumes on the rack in front of me, I am face to face with the romance and the beauty of another famous volume, which ſtands as a memorial of English domination in France.

Fashions change in illuminated manuscripts, as in all else, and books of hours were now beginning to be the vogue in place of psalters. This one was written and decorated for John, Duke of Bedford, son of Henry IV, and was probably a wedding gift to Anne, his wife. This marriage, it will be remembered, was intended to strengthen the English alliance with Anne's brother, Philip of Burgundy. On the blank page on the back of the Duke's portrait is a record in Latin, made by John Somerset, the King's physician, to the effect that on Chriſtmas Eve, 1430, the Duchess, with her husband's consent, presented the manuscript to the young King Henry VI, who was then at Rouen, on his way to be crowned at Paris. Such notes, made in these later illuminated volumes, are interesting as far as they go, but there is so much left unsaid! In the present instance, how came the manuscript, a hundred years later, in the possession of Henri II and Catherine de' Medici, of France? After being thus located, where was it for the next hundred years, before it was purchased by Edward Harley, 2d Earl of Oxford, from Sir Robert Worsley's widow, to be presented to his daughter, the Duchess of Portland? These are questions that naturally arise in one's mind as he turns the gorgeous pages, for it seems incredible that such beauty could remain hidden for such long periods. Now, happily, through purchase in 1852, the manuscript has reached its final resting place.

Like other books of hours, the *Bedford* opens with the Calendar pages, combining the signs of the Zodiac with beautifully executed scenes typical of each month. Then follow four full-page designs showing the Creation and Fall, the Building of the Ark, the Exit from the Ark, and the Tower of Babel. The Sequences of the Gospels come next; then the Hours of the Virgin, with Penitential Psalms and Litany; the Shorter Hours;

136

BEDFORD BOOK OF HOURS. *French,* 15th Century
Showing one of the superb Miniature Pages
(Brit. Mus. Add. MS. 18850. 10⅜ x 7¼ inches)

the Vigils of the Dead; the Fifteen Joys; the Hours of the Passion; the Memorials of the Saints; and various Prayers. Throughout the 289 leaves, a little larger than 10 by 7 inches, are thirty-eight full-page miniatures that are masterpieces,—particularly the Annunciation, with which the Hours of the Virgin begin. Every page of text is surrounded by a magnificent border, rich in colors and gold, with foliage and birds, and with the daintiest little miniatures imaginable. While these borders are based upon the ivy-leaf pattern, it resembles the style that carries the illumination through the leaf, bud, and flower up to the fruit itself, which one associates more with the Flemish than the French School. The work is really a combination of the French and Flemish Schools, but is essentially French in its conception and execution.

It was the custom, in these specially created manuscripts, to immortalize the heads of the family by including them with other, and, perhaps in some cases, more religious subjects. In this *Book of Hours*, the Duke of Bedford is depicted, clad in a long, fur-lined gown of cloth-of-gold, kneeling before Saint George, and the portrait is so fine that it has been frequently copied. The page which perpetuates the Duchess is reproduced here (at *page* 136). Clad in a sumptuous gown of cloth-of gold, lined with ermine, she kneels before Saint Anne; her elaborate head dress supports an artificial coiffure, rich in jewels; on her long train, her two favorite dogs are playing. The Saint is clad in a grey gown, with blue mantle and white veil, with an open book in front of her. At her left stands the Virgin in white, with jeweled crown, and the infant Christ, in grey robe. His mother has thrown her arm affectionately about Him, while He, in turn, beams on the kneeling Duchess. In His hand He carries an orb surmounted by a cross. Saint Joseph stands at the right of the background, and four angels may be seen with musical instruments, appearing above the arras, on which is stamped the device and motto of the Duchess.

Surrounding the miniature, worked into the border, in addition to the Duke's shield and arms, are exquisite smaller pictures, in architectural backgrounds, showing Saint Anne's three husbands and her sons in law. The pages must be seen in their full color, and in their original setting, to be appreciated.

The manuscript is bound in red velvet, with silver gilt clasps, bearing the Harley and the Cavendish arms, and dates back to the time of the Earl of Oxford.

ANTIQUITIES OF THE JEWS. *French Renaissance,* 15th Century
*Cyrus permits the Jews to return to their own Country, and to rebuild
the Temple of Jerusalem*
(Bibl. Nat. MS. François 247.   16¼ x 11½ inches)

THE LURE OF ILLUMINATION

In the *Antiquities of the Jews*, Jean Foucquet's masterpiece at the Bibliothèque Nationale in Paris, we find the French Renaissance School. This manuscript interests me for several and different reasons. In the first place, Foucquet was one of the founders of the French School of painting, and had his masterpieces been painted on canvas instead of on vellum, his name would have been much more familiar to art lovers than it is today. The high degree attained by the art at Tours, which had become the center of the Renaissance in France, demanded a setting for the miniatures different from the Flemish type of decoration that had so dominated illumination in general. This it found in the Italian style, which at that time was first attaining its glory.

The book itself was originally bound in two volumes, being a French translation by an unknown writer of Flavius Josephus' *Antiquities* and *War of the Jews*, the subject being the clemency of Cyrus toward the captive Jews in Babylon. It is in folio (a little larger than 16 by 11 inches), written in double column, and contains superb initials, vignettes, and miniatures (*page* 138). The work was begun for the Duc de Berry, but was left unfinished at his death in 1416. Later it came into the possession of the Duc de Nemours.

Can one imagine a more aristocratic treasure for a cultured gentleman to own! It was probably begun very early in the fifteenth century, and completed between the years 1455 and 1477. A note at the end of the first volume (which contains 311 leaves) by François Robertet, secretary of Pierre II, Duc de Bourbon, states that nine of the miniatures are "by the hand of that good painter of King Louis XI, Jean Foucquet, native of Tours."

For over two hundred years this first volume, containing Books I to XIV of the *Antiquities of the Jews*, has been in the Bibliothèque Nationale. It is bound in yellow morocco, and bears the arms of Louis XV. The second volume was considered lost. In 1903 the English collector, Mr. Henry Yates Thompson, purchased the missing copy in London, at a sale at Sotheby's. This contained Books XV to XX of the *Antiquities of the Jews* and Books I to VII of the *War of the Jews*; but it was imperfect in that a dozen pages of miniatures had been cut out. Two years later, Sir George Warner discovered ten of these filched leaves in an album of miniatures that at some time had been presented to Queen Victoria, and were in her collection at Windsor Castle.

As soon as Mr. Thompson heard of this discovery, he begged King Edward VII to accept his volume, in order that the leaves might be combined. The English monarch received the gift with the understanding that he, in turn, might present the restored manuscript to the President of the French Republic. This gracious act was accomplished on March 4, 1906, and now the two volumes rest side by side in the Bibliothèque Nationale, reunited for all time after their long separation. If books possess personalities, surely no international romance ever offered greater material for the novelist's imagination!

Now our pilgrimage takes us from Paris to Venice, to study that priceless treasure of the Library of San Marco, the *Grimani Breviary*, the gem of the Flemish School (which should properly be called "Netherlandish"). This style overlapped, distinctly, into Germany and France, and further complicated any certainty of identification by the fact that the number of Netherlandish illuminators was large, and they scattered themselves over Europe, practising their art and style in France, Germany, and Italy. They all worked with the same minute care, and it is practically impossible to identify absolutely the work even of the most famous artists. There has always been a question whether the chief glory of the *Grimani Breviary* belonged to Hans Memling or to Gerard Van-der-Meire, but from a study of the comparative claims the Memling enthusiasts would seem to have the better of the argument.

Internal and external evidence place the date of the execution of the *Grimani Breviary* at 1478 to 1489,—ten years being required for its completion. It is believed that the commission was given by Pope Sixtus IV. The Pontiff, however, died before the volume was finished, and it was left in the hands of one of the artists engaged upon it. Antonello di Messina purchased it from this artist, who is supposed to have been Hans Memling, and brought it to Venice, where he sold it for the sum of 500 ducats to Cardinal Domenico Grimani, whose name it bears.

This Cardinal Grimani was a man noted not only for his exemplary piety but also as a literary man of high repute, and a collector of rare judgment. When he died, the *Breviary* was bequeathed to his nephew, Marino Grimani, Patriarch of Aquileia, on the condition that at his death the precious manuscript should become the property of the Venetian Republic. Marino carried the *Breviary* with him to Rome, where it remained until his death in 1546. In spite of his precautions, however, this and several other valuable objects

GRIMANI BREVIARY. *Flemish*, 15th Century
La Vie au Mois de Janvier
(Biblioteca San Marco, Venice.   10 x 9 inches)

would have been irretrievably loſt had not Giovanni Grimani, Marino's successor as Patriarch
at Aquileia, searched for it, and finally recovered
it at great coſt to himself.

In recognition of his services, Venice granted
Giovanni the privilege of retaining the manuscript
in his possession during his lifetime. Faithful to
his truſt, Giovanni, fearing leſt the volume be
again loſt, on October 3, 1593, sent for his great
friend, Marco Antonio Barbaro, Procurator of
Saint Mark's, placed the treasure in his hands, and
charged him to deliver it to the Doge Pasquale
Cicogna in full Senate. This was done, and the
volume was ſtored in the Treasury of the Basilica
for safe keeping. Here it remained through the
many vicissitudes of Venice, and even after the
fall of the Republic, until the librarian Morelli
persuaded the authorities to allow its removal
to the Library of San Marco, whither it was
transferred October 4, 1797.

When the *Breviary* was delivered to the Doge
Pasquale, the Republic voted to entruſt the binding
to one Alessandro Vittoria. The cover is of crimson velvet, largely hidden by ornaments of silver
gilt. On one side are the arms and the medallion
of Cardinal Domenico Grimani, and on the other
those of his father, the Doge Antonio. Both

covers contain further decorations and Latin in-
scriptions, relating in the first case to the gift, and
in the other to its confirmation. In the small
medallions in the border one sees a branch of
laurel, the emblem of vigilance and protection,
crossed by a branch of palm,—the symbol of
the religious life. The dove typifies purity, and
the dragon stands for defense.

The volume itself contains 831 pages about
10 by 9 inches in size. There are the usual Calendar pages, containing the signs of the Zodiac,
and further decorated with small miniatures (*opp.
page*), alternating with twelve superb full-page
illuminations (*page* 142), showing the occupations of the months. Following these, come the
Prayers, with sixty additional full-page miniatures
based on Bible history or the lives of the Saints.
At the end are eighteen pages with smaller miniatures assigned to the saints of special devotion,
placed at the beginning of the office dedicated to
each.

The marginal decorations throughout the book
are wonderfully wrought. Some pages are adorned
with perpendicular bands, with constantly varying color combinations. Arabesques of all kinds
are used, and interspersed among the ornamenta-
tion are flowers and fruits, animals, birds, fishes,

144

GRIMANI BREVIARY. *Flemish,* 15th Century
Text Page showing Miniature and Decoration
(Biblioteca San Marco, Venice. 10 x 9 inches)

and all kinds of natural objects. In addition to these, one finds little buildings, landscapes, archi- tectural ornaments, statues, church ornaments, frames, vases, cameos, medals, and scenes from Bible history and from every-day life as well,— all showing the genius of the artists who put them- selves into the spirit of their work.

When the old Campanile fell in 1902, one corner of the Library of San Marco was damaged. Immediately telegrams poured in from all over the world, anxiously inquiring for the safety of the *Grimani Breviary*. Fortunately it was untouched. The last time I saw this precious manuscript was in 1924. Doctor Luigi Ferrari, the librarian, courteously took the volume from its case and laid it tenderly on a low table, extending to me the unusual privilege of personal examination. Thus I could turn the pages slowly enough to enjoy again the exquisite charm of its miniatures, the beauty of its coloring, and to assimilate the depth of feeling which pervades it throughout. My friends at the British Museum think that in the Flemish pages of the *Sforza Book of Hours* they have the finest example of the Flemish School. They may be right; but no miniatures I have ever seen have seemed to me more marvelously beautiful than those in the *Grimani Breviary*.

Whenever I examine a beautiful manuscript, and take delight in it, I find myself comparing it with the Italian masterpiece of Francesco d'Antonio del Cherico. It may be that this is due to my dramatic introduction to that volume, as recorded at the beginning of this chapter. Its date is perhaps half a century earlier than the *Hours of Anne of Brittany*; it is of the same period as the *Grimani Breviary* and the *Antiquities of the Jews*; it is fifty years later than the *Bedford Book of Hours*, and a century and a half later than *Queen Mary's Psalter*. Which of all these magnificent manuscripts is the most beautiful? Who would dare to say! In all there is found the expression of art in its highest form; in each the individual admirer finds some special feature—the beauty of the designs, the richness of the composition, the warmth of the coloring, or the perfection of the execution—that particularly appeals.

When one considers the early civilization of Italy, and the heights finally attained by Italian illuminators, it is difficult to understand why the intervening centuries show such tardy recognition of the art. Even as late as the twelfth century, with other countries turning out really splendid examples, the Italian work is of a distinctly inferior order; but by the middle of the thirteenth

BOOK OF HOURS. *Italian,* 15th Century
By Francesco d'Antonio del Cherico
(R. Lau. Bibl. Ashb. 1874. 7 x 5 inches)

century, the great revival in art brought about by Cimabue and Giotto ſtimulated the development in illumination. During the next hundred years the art became nationalized. The ornament diverged from the French type, and assumed the peculiar ſtraight bar or rod, with profile foliages, and the sudden reversions of the curves with change of color, which are characteriſtic of fourteenth-century Italian work. The miniatures, introducing the new Tuscan manner of painting, entirely re-fashioned miniature art. The figure becomes natural, well-proportioned, and graceful, the heads delicate in feature and correct in expression. The coſtumes are carefully wrought, the drapery folds soft, yet elaborately finished. The colors are vivid but warm, the blue being particularly effective.

The vine-ſtem ſtyle immediately preceded the Classic revival which came when the Medici and other wealthy patrons recognized the artiſtic importance of illumination. In this ſtyle the ſtems are coiled moſt gracefully, slightly tinted, with decorative flowerets. The grounds are marked by varying colors, in which the artiſts delicately traced tendrils in gold or white.

The great glory of Italy in illumination came after the invention of printing. Aside from the

apprehensions of the wealthy owners of manu/
script libraries that they would lose prestige if
books became common, beyond the danger to the
high/born rulers of losing their political power
if the masses learned argument from the printed
book,—these true lovers of literature opposed the
printing press because they believed it to cheapen
something that was so precious as to demand
protection. So they vied with one another in
encouraging the scribes and the illuminators to
produce hand/written volumes such as had never
before been seen.

Certainly the *Book of Hours* of d'Antonio is one
of the marvels of Florentine art. The nine full/
page miniatures have never been surpassed. No
wonder that Lorenzo de' Medici, lover of the
beautiful, should have kept it ever beside him!
The delicate work in the small scenes in the
Calendar is as precise as that in the larger minia/
tures; the decoration, rich in the variety of its
design, really surpassed the splendor and glory of
the goldsmith's art (*page* 146). Some deplore the
fact that England lost this treasure when the
Italian government purchased the Ashburnham
Collection in 1884; but if there ever was a manu/
script that belongs in Florence, it is this.

You may still see d'Antonio's masterpiece at

HOURS of ANNE of BRITTANY. *French Renaissance,* 16th Century
The Education of the Child Jesus by the Virgin and Saint Joseph
(Bibl. Nat. MS. Lat. 9474.   12 x 7½ inches)

the Laurenziana Library, but it is no longer kept in the ancient wooden desk. The treasures of illu-mination are now splendidly arrayed in cases, where all may study and admire. There are heavy choir-books, classic manuscripts, books of hours, and breviaries, embellished by Lorenzo Monaco, master of Fra Angelico; by Benozzo Gozzoli, whose frescoes still make the Riccardi famous; by Gherado, and Clovio, and by other artists whose names have long since been forgotten, but whose work remains as an everlasting monument to a departed art that should be revived.

Experts, I believe, place the work of Jean Foucquet, in the *Antiquities of the Jews*, ahead of that of Jean Bourdichon (probably Foucquet's pupil) in the *Hours of Anne of Brittany*; but frankly this sixteenth century manuscript at the Bibliothèque Nationale, in Paris, always yields me greater pleasure. Perhaps this is in compensa-tion for not knowing too much! I will agree with them that the decorative borders of Foucquet are much more interesting than Bourdichon's, for the return of the Flemish influence to French art at this time was not particularly fortunate. In the borders of the *Grimani Breviary* realism in re-producing flowers, vegetables, bugs, and small animal life, would seem to have been carried to the limit, but Bourdichon went the *Grimani* one better, and on a larger scale. The reproductions are marvelously exact, but even a beautifully painted domesticated onion, on which a dragon-fly crawls, with wing so delicately transparent that one may read the letter it seems to cover, is a curious accompaniment for the magnificently executed portraits of Anne and her patron saints in the miniature pages! Here the artist has succeeded in imparting a quality to his work that makes it appear as if done on ivory instead of vellum (see *page* 148). The costumes and even the jewels are brilliant in the extreme. The floral decorations shown in the reproduction opposite are far more decorative than the vegetables, but I still object to the caterpillar and the bugs!

In 1508 there is a record that Anne of Brittany, Queen of Louis XII, made an order of payment to Bourdichon of 1050 *livres tournois* for his services in "richly and sumptuously historiating and illuminating a great Book of Hours for our use." This consists of 238 leaves of vellum, 12 by 7½ inches in size. There are sixty-three full pages, including forty-nine miniatures, twelve reproductions for the various months, and a leaf containing ornaments and figures at the beginning

HOURS of ANNE of BRITTANY. *French Renaissance, 16th Century*
Page showing Text and Marginal Decoration
(Bibl. Nat. MS. Lat. 9474. 12 x 7¼ inches)

and end of the volume. Of the text, there are some 350 pages surrounded by borders. The Italian influence shows in the architectural and sculptural decorations, just as the Flemish obtains in the borders.

The manuscript is bound in black shagreen, with chased silver clasps.

The question naturally arises as to the reason for the decline and practically the final extinction of the art. I believe it to be that which the princely Italian patrons foresaw. Their apprehensions, though selfish in motive, have been confirmed by history. The invention of printing did make the book common, and as such, its true significance came to be forgotten because of greater familiarity. The book as the developer of the people in science and in literature crowded out the book as an expression of art.

I wonder if it is too late to revive illumination. Never has there existed in America or England a keener appreciation of beautiful books; never have there been so many lovers of the book blessed with the financial ability to gratify their tastes. There are still artists familiar with the art, who, if encouraged, could produce work worthy of the beautifully printed volumes the best Presses are capable of turning out. What is lacking is simply a realization that illumination stands side by side with art at its best. In America, the opportunities for studying illumination are restricted, but a student would have no difficulty in finding in certain private collections and in a few public libraries more than enough to establish his basic understanding of the art. The great masterpieces are permanently placed now, and strictly enforced laws prevent national monuments from being further transferred from one country to another; but even of these, excellent facsimile reproductions have been made and distributed throughout the world

No true lover of art visits Europe without first preparing himself by reading and study for a fuller understanding and more perfect enjoyment of what he is to find in the various galleries. Assuming that no one can be an art lover without also being a lover of books, it is perhaps a fair question to ask why he should not make an equal effort to prepare himself to understand and enjoy those rich treasures in the art of illumination which are now so easily accessible

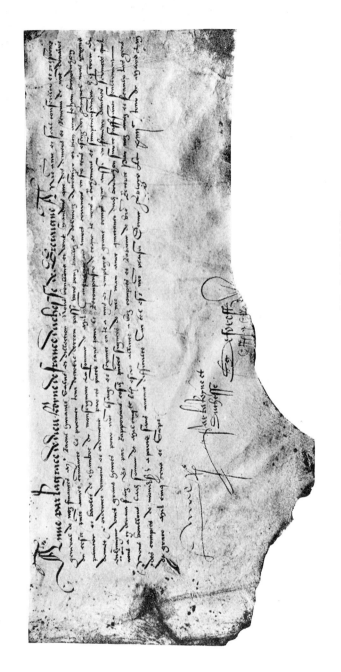

HOURS OF ANNE OF BRITTANY

Order of payment of 1050 *livres tournois* to Jean Bourdichon, 1508

CHAPTER V
Friends through the Pen

V

FRIENDS THROUGH THE PEN

MAURICE HEWLETT combined to an unusual degree those salient characteristics that go to make the great writer: he was a discerning observer, and had formed the habit of analyzing what he observed; his personal experiences had taught him the significance of what he had seen and enabled him to assess its valuation. Beyond all,—having observed, analyzed, and understood, —he possessed the power to interpret to others.

At the time I first met him, *The Queen's Quair* was having a tremendous run, and the volume naturally came into the conversation.

"In spite of its success," he said with much feeling, "I am disappointed over its reception. I have always wanted to write history, but not the way history has always been written. There are certain acts attributed to the chief characters which, if these characters are studied analytically, are obviously impossible; yet because a certain event has once been recorded it keeps on being repeated and magnified until history itself becomes a series of distortions. Mary, Queen of Scots, has always been my favorite historical figure, and I know that in *The Queen's Quair* I have given a truer picture of her character than any that at present exists. But alas," he added with a sigh, " no one accepts it as other than fiction."

After this statement from him I turned again to my copy of *The Queen's Quair* and reread the author's prologue, in which I found:

A hundred books have been written and a hundred songs sung; men enough of these latter days have broken their hearts over Queen Mary's; what is more to the point is that no heart but hers was broken at the time. All the world can love her now, but who loved her then? Not a man among them. A few girls went weeping; a few boys laid down their necks that she might fall free of the mire. Alas, the mire swallowed them up and she needs must conceal her pretty feet. This is the note of the tragedy; pity is involved, rather than terror. But no song ever pierced the fold of her secret, no book ever found out the truth because none ever sought her heart. Here, then, is a book which has sought nothing else, and a song which springs from that only.

I wonder if every writer in his heart does not feel the same ambition. The novelist is a story-teller who recites bed-time stories to his audience of

156

grown-up children, while the humorist plays the clown; but in writing history one is dealing with something basic. Within a year a volume has been published containing alleged documentary evidence to prove that Mary, Queen of Scots, was innocent of the charge of treason. What a triumph if an author through character analysis could correct tradition! It was a loss to the world that Hewlett permitted himself to be discouraged by unsympathetic critics from carrying out a really big idea.

To meet Maurice Hewlett at his home at Broad Chalke, a little English village nearly ten miles from a railroad station, and to walk with him in his garden, one might recognize the author of *The Forest Lovers*; but an afternoon with him at a London club would develop another side which was less himself. Instead of discussing flowers and French memoirs and biography in a delightfully whimsical mood, Hewlett's slight, wiry figure became tense, his manner alert, his eyes keen and watchful. In the country he was the dreamer, the bohemian, wholly detached from the world outside; in the city he was confident and determined in approaching any subject, his voice became crisp and decisive, his bearing was that of the man of the world.

His early life was more or less unhappy, due partly to his precociousness which prevented him from fitting in with youth of his own age. This encouraged him to reach beyond his strength and thus find disappointment.

"I was never a boy," he said once, "except possibly after the time when I should have been a man. As I look back on my youth, it was filled with discouragements."

The classics fascinated him, and he absorbed Dante. Then Shelley and Keats shared the place of the Italian poet in his heart. Even after he married, he continued to gratify his love of Bohemia, and his wife wandered with him through Italy, with equal joy; while in England they camped out together in the New Forest, — the scene of *The Forest Lovers*.

The peculiar style which Hewlett affected in many of his volumes resulted, he told me, from his daily work in the Record Office in London, as Keeper of Land Revenue Records and Enrolments, during which period he studied the old parchments, dating back to William the Conqueror. In this respect his early experience was not unlike that of Austin Dobson's, and just as the work in the Harbours Department failed to kill Dobson's poetic *finesse*, so did Hewlett rise above

158

the deadly grind of ancient records and archives. In fact it was during this period that Hewlett produced *Pan and the Young Shepherd*, which contains no traces of its author's archaic environment.

One point of sympathy that drew us closely together was our mutual love for Italy. My first desire to know Maurice Hewlett better was after reading his *Earthwork Out of Tuscany*, *Little Novels of Italy*, and *The Road in Tuscany*. I have always preferred these volumes to any of his later ones, as to me they have seemed more spontaneous and more genuine expressions of himself. We were talking about Italy, one day, when he made a remark which caused me to suggest that what he said was the expression of a modern humanist. Hewlett was obviously surprised yet pleased by my use of this expression.

" I don't often meet any one interested in the subject of humanism," he said. " It is one of my hobbies."

I explained my association with Doctor Guido Biagi, librarian of the Laurenziana Library at Florence, and the work I had done there in connection with my designs for a special face of type, based upon the beautiful hand letters of the humanistic scribes (see *page* 16). With that introduction we discussed the great importance of the

humanistic movement as the forerunner and essence
of the Renaissance. We talked of Petrarch, the
father of humanism, and of the courageous fight
he and his sturdy band of followers made to rescue
the classics. We both had recently read Philippe
Monnier's *Le Quattrocento*, which gave additional
interest to our discussion.

"Monnier is the only writer I have ever read
who has tried to define humanism," Hewlett continued. "He says it is not only the love of antiquity, but the worship of it,—a worship carried
so far that it is not limited to adoration alone, but
which forces one to reproduce."

"And the humanist," I added, picking up the
quotation from Monnier, which I knew by heart,
" is not only the man who knows intimately the
ancients and is inspired by them; it is he who is
so fascinated by their magic spell that he copies
them, imitates them, rehearses their lessons, adopts
their models and their methods, their examples
and their gods, their spirit and their tongue."

"Well, well!" he laughed; "we *have* struck
the same street, haven't we! But does that exactly
express the idea to you? It isn't antiquity we
worship, but rather the basic worth for which
the ancients stand."

"Monnier refers to the obsession that comes

7, Northwick Terrace, N.W.

26 Nov. 1905

Dear Mr Orcutt,

I've said my little
say about Twelfth Night
and enclose it herewith.
I hope you will approve.

I also return your Laugh's
and Dobson's prefaces.
I like Laug's the better of
the two — excellent.

My best regards to Mrs
Orcutt

Yours try

M. Hewlett.

Autograph Letter from Maurice Hewlett

from constant contact with the learning of the past, and the atmosphere thus created," I replied. "Only last year Biagi and I discussed that very point, sitting together in his luxuriant garden at Castiglioncello, overlooking the Gulf of Leghorn. The 'basic worth' you mention is really Truth, and taking this as a starting point, we worked out a modern application of Monnier's definition:

" *The humanist is one who holds himself open to receive Truth, unprejudiced as to its source, and, after having received Truth, realizes his obligation to give it out again, made richer by his personal interpretation.*"

"There is a definition with a present applica⁄tion," Hewlett exclaimed heartily. "I like it.— Did you have that in mind when you called me a modern humanist, just now?"

"No one could read *Earthwork Out of Tuscany* and think otherwise," I insisted.

Hewlett held out his hand impulsively. "I wish I might accept that compliment with a clear conscience," he demurred.

Meeting Austin Dobson after he became in⁄terpreter⁄in⁄chief of the eighteenth century, it was difficult to associate him with his earlier experi⁄ences as a clerk in the Board of Trade office, which he entered when he was sixteen years old, and to which service he devoted forty-five useful but uneventful years, rising eventually to be a principal in the Harbours Department. With so quiet and unassuming a personality, it seems incredible that he could have lifted himself bodily from such unimaginative environment, and, through his classic monographs, bring Steele, Goldsmith, Richardson, Fielding, Horace Walpole, Fanny Burney, Bewick, and Hogarth, out of their hazy indefiniteness, and give to them such living reality. Perhaps Dobson's very nature prevented him from seeing the coarseness and indecency of the period, and enabled him to introduce, or perhaps reintroduce, to England from France the *ballade* and the *chante royal*, the *rondeau* and the *rondel*, the *triolet*, the *villanelle*, and other fascinating but obsolete poetical forms in which he first became interested through his French grandmother.

Dobson was the most modest literary man I ever met. I happened to be in London at the time when the English government bestowed upon him an annuity of £1,000, " for distinguished service to the crown." When I congratulated him upon this honor his response was characteristic:

" I don't know why in the world they have given me this, unless it is because I am the father of ten children. I have no doubt that would be classified under 'distinguished service to the crown.'"

One afternoon Austin Dobson and Richard Garnett, then Keeper of the Printed Books at the British Museum, happened to come to my hotel in London for tea at the same time. On a table in the apartment was a two-volume quarto edition in French of *Don Quixote*, a prize I had unearthed at a bookstall on the Quai Voltaire in Paris. It was beautifully printed, the letterpress just biting into the paper, and making itself a part of the leaf, which is so characteristic of the best French presswork. The edition also contained the famous Doré illustrations. Dobson picked up one of the volumes and exclaimed over its beauty.

" This edition," he said, " is absolutely perfect."

" Not quite," I qualified his statement. " It is lacking in one particular. It requires your *Ode to Cervantes* to make it complete."

Dobson laughed. " Send the book to me," he said, " and I will transcribe the lines on the fly leaf."

When the volume was returned a few days later, a letter of apology came with it. " When I copied out the *Ode* on the fly leaf," Dobson wrote, "it looked so lost on the great page that I ventured to add the poem which I composed for the tercentenary. I hope you won't mind."

My eleven-year-old son came into the reception room while our guests were drinking their tea. Dobson took him on his lap, and after quite winning his affection by his gentleness, he quietly called his attention to Garnett, who was conversing with my wife in another part of the room.

"Never forget that man, my boy," Dobson said in a low voice. "We have never had in England, nor shall we ever have again, one who knows so much of English literature. If the record of every date and every fact were to be lost by fire, Garnett could reproduce them with absolute accuracy if his life were spared long enough."

Within fifteen minutes the youngster found himself on Garnett's knee. Without knowing what Dobson had said, the old man whispered in the child's ear, "It is a privilege you will be glad to remember that you have met such a man as Austin Dobson. Except for Salisbury's desire to demean the post of poet laureate, Dobson would hold that position today. Never forget that you have met Austin Dobson."

A few months after our return to America, Garnett died, and Dobson sent me the following lines. I have never known of their publication:

IN QUEST OF THE PERFECT BOOK

RICHARD GARNETT

Sit tibi terra levis

Of him we may say justly: Here was one
Who knew of most things more than any other,—
Who loved all Learning underneath the sun,
And looked on every Learner as a brother.

Nor was this all. For those who knew him, knew,
However far his love's domain extended,
It held its quiet " poet's corner," too,
Where Mirth, and Song, and Irony, were blended.

Garnett was a rare spirit, and the British Museum has never seemed the same since he retired in
1899. Entrance to his private office was cleverly
concealed by a door made up of shelf-backs of
books, but once within the sanctum the genial
host placed at the disposal of his guest, in a matter-
of-fact way, such consummate knowledge as to
stagger comprehension. But, far beyond this, the
charm of his personality will always linger in the
minds of those who knew him, and genuine affection for the man will rival the admiration for his
scholarship.

One afternoon at Ealing, after tennis on the
lawn behind the Dobson house, we gathered for
tea. Our little party included Hugh Thomson,

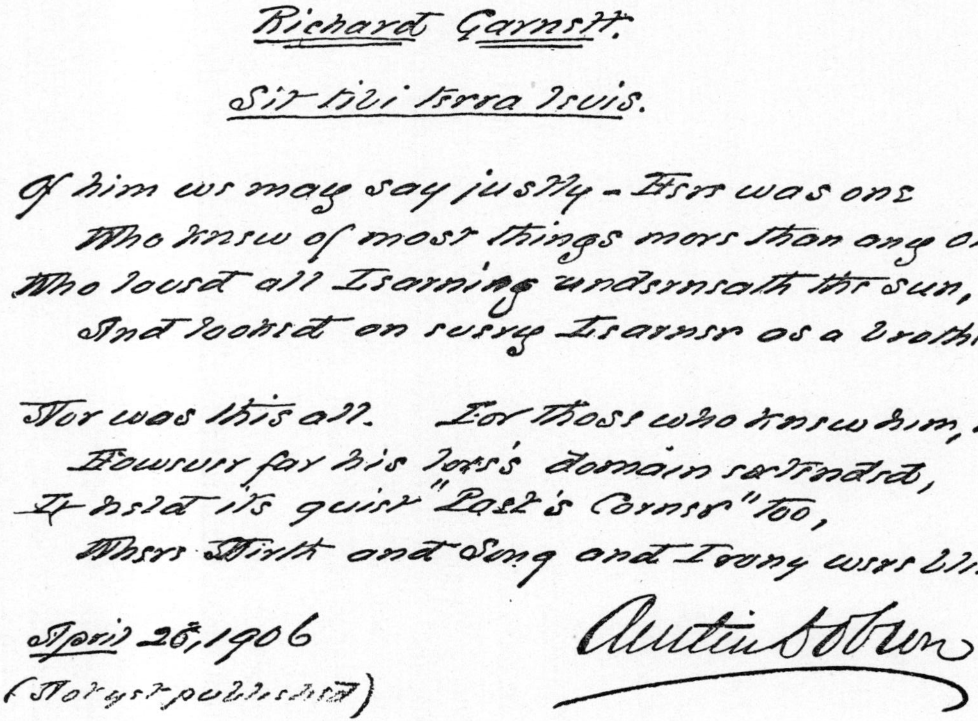

Autograph Poem by Austin Dobson

the artist who so charmingly illustrated much of
Dobson's work, Mr. and Mrs. Dobson, and one
of his sons. The poet was in his most genial mood,
and the conversation led us into mutually con-
fidential channels.

"I envy you your novel writing," he said.
"Fiction gives one so much wider scope, and
prose is so much more satisfactory as a medium
than poetry. I have always wanted to write a
novel. Mrs. Dobson would never have it. But
she is always right," he added; "had I persisted
I should undoubtedly have lost what little reputation I have."

He was particularly impressed by the fact that
I wrote novels as an avocation. It seemed to him
such a far cry from the executive responsibility of
a large business, and he persisted in questioning
me as to my methods. I explained that I devoted a
great deal of time to creating mentally the characters who would later demand my pen; that with
the general outline of the plot I intended to develop,
I approached it exactly as a theatrical manager approaches a play he is about to produce, spending
much time in selecting my cast, adding, discard-
ing, changing, just so far as seemed to me necessary
to secure the actors best suited to the parts I planned
to have them play. He expressed surprise when I

told him that I had long since discarded the idea of working out a definite scenario, depending rather upon creating interesting characters, and having them sufficiently alive so that when placed together under interesting circumstances they are bound to produce interesting dialogue and action.

"Of course my problem, writing essays and poetry, is quite different from yours as a novelist," he said; "but I do try to assume a relation toward my work that is objective and impersonal. In a way, I go farther than you do."

Then he went on to say that not only did he plan the outline of what he had to write, whether triolet or poem, wholly in his head, but (in the case of the poetry) even composed the lines and made the necessary changes before having recourse to pen and paper.

"When I actually begin to write," he said, " I can see the lines clearly before me, even to the interlinear corrections, and it is a simple matter for me to copy them out in letter-perfect form."

Dobson's handwriting and his signature were absolutely dissimilar. Unless one had actually seen him transcribe the text of a letter or the lines of a poem in that beautiful designed script, he would think it the work of some one other than the writer of the flowing autograph beneath.

IN QUEST OF THE PERFECT BOOK

Posterity is now deciding whether Mark Twain's fame will rest upon his humor or his philosophy, yet his continuing popularity would seem to have settled this much-mooted question. Humor is fleeting unless based upon real substance. In life the passing quip that produces a smile serves its purpose, but to bring to the surface such human notes as dominate Mark Twain's stories, a writer must possess extraordinary powers of observation and a complete understanding of his fellow man. Neither Tom Sawyer nor Huckleberry Finn is a fictional character, but is rather the personification of that leaven which makes life worth living.

When an author has achieved the dignity of having written "works" rather than books, he has placed himself in the hands of his friends in all his varying moods. A single volume is but the fragment of any writer's personality. I have laughed over *Innocents Abroad,* and other volumes which helped to make Mark Twain's reputation, but when I seek a volume to recall the author as I knew him best it is *Joan of Arc* that I always take down from the shelf. This book really shows the side of Mark Twain, the man, as his friends knew him, yet it was necessary to publish the volume anony-mously in order to secure for it consideration from the reading public as a serious story.

170

MARK TWAIN, 1835-1910
At the Villa di Quarto, Florence
From a Snap-shot

" No one will ever accept it seriously, over my signature," Mark Twain said. " People always want to laugh over what I write. This is a serious book. It means more to me than anything I have ever undertaken."

Mark Twain was far more the humorist when off guard than when on parade. The originality of what he did, combined with what he said, produced the maximum expression of himself. At one time he and his family occupied the Villa di Quarto in Florence (*page* 172), and while in Italy Mrs. Orcutt and I were invited to have tea with them. The villa is located, as its name suggests, in the four-mile radius from the center of the town. It was a large, unattractive building, perhaps fifty feet wide and four times as long. The location was superb, looking out over Florence toward Vallombrosa and the Chianti hills.

In greeting us, Mark Twain gave the impression of having planned out exactly what he was going to say. I had noticed the same thing on other occasions. He knew that people expected him to say something humorous or unusual, and he tried not to disappoint them.

"Welcome to the barracks," he exclaimed. "Looks like a hotel, doesn't it? You'd think with twenty bedrooms on the top floor and only four in my family there would be a chance to put up a friend or two, wouldn't you? But there isn't any one I think so little of as to be willing to stuff him into one of those cells."

We had tea out of doors. Miss Clara Clemens, who later became Mrs. Gabrilowitch, served as hostess, as Mrs. Clemens was confined to her bed by the heart trouble that had brought the family to Italy. As we sipped our tea and nibbled at the delicious Italian cakes, Mark Twain continued his comments on the villa, explaining that it was alleged to have been built by the first Cosimo de' Medici ("If it was, he had a bum architect," Mark Twain interjected); later it was occupied by the King of Würtemberg ("He was the genius who put in the Pullman staircase"); and still later by a Russian Princess ("She is responsible for that green majolica stove in the hall. When I first saw it I thought it was a church for children"); and then it fell into the hands of his landlady ("Less said about her the better. You never heard such profanity as is expressed by the furniture and the carpets she put in to complete the misery. I'm always thankful when darkness comes on to stop the swearing").

The garden was beautiful, but oppressive, — due probably to the tall cypresses (always funereal in

Villa di Quarto
Firenze

Dear Mr. & Mrs. Orcutt:

They are superb —
the most extraordinary
flowers I have ever
seen — & Mrs. Clemens
being too very ill to
see, I thank them & for
your kind remem-
brance; & in this
the rest of us join,
with best wishes

for your both & to
cordial Adjuvie —
Yorschen!

S. Clemens

AUTOGRAPH LETTER FROM MARK TWAIN
With Snapshot of Villa di Quarto

their aspect), which kept out the sun, and pro‑
duced a mouldy luxuriance. The marble seats and
statues were covered with green moss, and the ivy
ran riot over everything. One felt the antiquity
unpleasantly, and, in a way, it seemed an unfortu‑
nate atmosphere for an invalid. But so far as the
garden was concerned, it made little difference
to Mrs. Clemens,—the patient, long‑suffering
"Livy" of Mark Twain's life,—for she never left
her sick chamber, and died three days later.

After tea, Mr. Clemens offered me a cigar and
watched me while I lighted it.

"Hard to get good cigars over here," he re‑
marked. "I'm curious to know what you think
of that one."

I should have been sorry to tell him what my
opinion really was, but I continued to smoke it
with as cheerful an expression as possible.

"What kind of cigars do you smoke while in
Europe?" he inquired.

I told him that I was still smoking a brand I had
brought over from America, and at the same time
I offered him one, which he promptly accepted,
throwing away the one he had just lighted. He
puffed with considerable satisfaction, and then
asked,

"How do you like that cigar I gave you?"

It seemed a matter of courtesy to express more enthusiasm than I really felt.

"Clara," he called across to where the ladies were talking, "Mr. Orcutt likes these cigars of mine, and he's a judge of good cigars."

Then turning to me he continued, "Clara says they're rotten!"

He relapsed into silence for a moment.

"How many of those cigars of yours have you on your person at the present time?"

I opened my cigar case, and disclosed four.

"I'll tell you what I'll do," he said suddenly. "You like my cigars and I like yours. I'll swap you even!"

In the course of the afternoon Mark Twain told of a dinner that Andrew Carnegie had given in his New York home, at which Mr. Clemens had been a guest. He related with much detail how the various speakers had stammered and halted, and seemed to find themselves almost tongue-tied. His explanation of this was their feeling of embarrassment because of the presence of only one woman, Mrs. Carnegie.

Sir Sidney Lee, who was lecturing on Shakesperian subjects in America at the time, was the guest of honor. When dinner was announced, Carnegie sent for Archie, the piper, an important feature in the Carnegie *ménage,* who appeared in full kilts, and led the procession into the dining-room, playing on the pipes. Carnegie, holding Sir Sidney's hand, followed directly after, giving an imitation of a Scotch dance, while the other guests fell in behind, matching the steps of their leader as closely as possible. Mark Twain gave John Burroughs credit for being the most success-ful in this attempt.

Some weeks later, at a dinner which Sir Sidney Lee gave in our honor in London, we heard an echo of this incident. Sir Sidney included the story of Mark Twain's speech on that occasion, which had been omitted in the earlier narrative. When called upon, Mr. Clemens had said,

"I'm not going to make a speech,—I'm just going to reminisce. I'm going to tell you some-thing about our host here when he didn't have as much money as he has now. At that time I was the editor of a paper in a small town in Connecti-cut, and one day, when I was sitting in the editorial sanctum, the door opened and who should come in but Andrew Carnegie. Do you remember that day, Andy?" he inquired, turning to his host; "wasn't it a scorcher?"

Carnegie nodded, and said he remembered it perfectly.

" Well," Mark Twain continued, "Andrew took off his hat, mopped his brow, and sat down in a chair, looking most disconsolate.

"'What's the matter?' I inquired. 'What makes you so melancholy?'—Do you remember that, Andy?" he again appealed to his host.

"Oh, yes," Carnegie replied, smiling broadly; "I remember it as if it were yesterday."

"'I am so sad,' Andy answered, 'because I want to found some libraries, and I haven't any money. I came in to see if you could lend me a million or two.' I looked in the drawer and found that I could let him have the cash just as well as not, so I gave him a couple of million.—Do you remember that, Andy?"

"No!" Carnegie answered vehemently; "I don't remember that at all!"

"That's just the point," Mark Twain continued, shaking his finger emphatically. "I have never received one cent on that loan, interest or principal!"

I wonder if so extraordinary an assemblage of literary personages was ever before gathered together as at the seventieth anniversary birthday dinner given to Mark Twain by Colonel George Harvey at Delmonico's in New York! Seated at the various tables were such celebrities as William

FRIENDS THROUGH THE PEN

Dean Howells, George W. Cable, Brander Matthews, Richard Watson Gilder, Kate Douglas
Wiggin, F. Hopkinson Smith, Agnes Repplier,
Andrew Carnegie, and Hamilton W. Mabie.

It was a long dinner. Every one present would
have been glad to express his affection and admiration for America's greatest manofletters, and
those who must be heard were so numerous that
it was nearly two o'clock in the morning before
Mark Twain's turn arrived to respond. As he
rose, the entire company rose with him, each standing on his chair and waving his napkin enthusiastically. Mark Twain was visibly affected by the
outburst of enthusiasm. When the excitement
subsided, I could see the tears streaming down his
cheeks, and all thought of the set speech he had
prepared and sent to the press for publication was
entirely forgotten. Realizing that the following
quotation differs from the official report of the
event, I venture to rely upon the notes I personally made during the dinner. Regaining control
of himself, Mark Twain began his remarks with
words to this effect:

*When I think of my first birthday and compare it with
this celebration, —just a bare room; no one present but
my mother and one other woman; no flowers, no wine, no
cigars, no enthusiasm, —I am filled with indignation!*

177

IN QUEST OF THE PERFECT BOOK

Charles Eliot Norton is a case in point in my contention that to secure the maximum from a college course a man should take two years at eighteen and the remaining two after he has reached forty. I was not unique among the Harvard undergraduates flocking to attend his courses in Art who failed utterly to understand or appreciate him. The ideals expressed in his lectures were far over our heads. The estimate of Carlyle, Ruskin, and Matthew Arnold, that Mr. Norton was foremost among American thinkers, scholars, and men of culture, put us on the defensive, for to have writers such as these include Norton as one of themselves placed him entirely outside the pale of our undergraduate understanding. He seemed to us a link connecting our generation with the distant past. As I look back upon it, this was not so much because he appeared old as it was that what he said seemed to our untrained minds the vagaries of age. Perhaps we were somewhat in awe of him, as we knew him to be the intimate of Oliver Wendell Holmes and James Russell Lowell, as he had been of Longfellow and George William Curtis, and thus the last of the Cambridge Immortals. I have always wished that others might have corrected their false impressions by learning to know Norton, the man, as I came to know him, and have

178

enjoyed the inspiring friendship that I was so fortunate in having him, in later years, extend to me.

In the classroom, sitting on a small, raised plat-
form, with as many students gathered before him
as the largest room in Massachusetts Hall could
accommodate, he took Art as a text and discussed
every subject beneath the sun. His voice, though
low, had a musical quality which carried to the
most distant corner. As he spoke he leaned forward on his elbows with slouching shoulders,
with his keen eyes passing constantly from one part
of the room to another, seeking, no doubt, some
gleam of understanding from his hearers. He told
me afterwards that it was not art he sought to teach,
nor ethics, nor philosophy, but that he would
count it success if he instilled in the hearts of even
a limited number of his pupils a desire to seek
the truth.

As I think of the Norton I came to know in the
years that followed, he seems to be a distinctly
different personality, yet of course the difference
was in me. Even at the time when Senator Hoar
made his terrific attack upon him for his public
utterances against the Spanish War, I knew that
he was acting true to his high convictions, even
though at variance with public opinion. I differed
from him, but by that time I understood him.

"Shady Hill," his home in Norton's Woods on the outskirts of Cambridge, Massachusetts, exuded the personality of its owner more than any house I was ever in. There was a restful dignity and stately culture, a courtly hospitality that reflected the individuality of the host. The library was the inner shrine. Each volume was selected for its own special purpose, each picture was illustrative of some special epoch, each piece of furniture performed its exact function. Here, unconsciously, while discussing subjects far afield, I acquired from Mr. Norton a love of Italy which later was fanned into flame by my Tuscan friend, Doctor Guido Biagi, the accomplished librarian of the Laurenziana Library, in Florence, to whom I have already frequently referred.

Our real friendship began when I returned from Italy in 1902, and told him of my plans to design a type based upon the wonderful humanistic volumes. As we went over the photographs and sketches I brought home with me, and he realized that a fragment of the fifteenth century, during which period hand lettering had reached its highest point of perfection, had actually been overlooked by other type designers (see *page* 16), he displayed an excitement I had never associated with his personality. I was somewhat excited, too, in being able to tell him something which had not previously come to his attention, — of the struggle of the Royal patrons, who tried to thwart the new-born art of printing by showing what a miserable thing a printed book was when compared with the beauty of the hand letters; and that these humanistic volumes, whose pages I had photographed, were the actual books which these patrons had ordered the scribes to produce, regardless of expense, to accomplish their purpose.

The romance that surrounded the whole undertaking brought out from him comments and discussion in which he demonstrated his many-sided personality. The library at "Shady Hill" became a veritable Florentine rostrum. Mr. Norton's sage comments were expressed with the vigor and originality of Politian; when he spoke of the tyranny of the old Florentine despots and compared them with certain political characters in our own America, he might have been Machiavelli uttering his famous diatribes against the State. Lorenzo de' Medici himself could not have thrilled me more with his fascinating expression of the beautiful or the exhibition of his exquisite taste.

Each step in the development of the Humanistic type was followed by Mr. Norton with the deepest interest. When the first copy of Petrarch's

Triumphs came through the bindery I took it to "Shady Hill," and we went over it page by page, from cover to cover. As we closed the volume he looked up with that smile his friends so loved,— that smile Ruskin called "the sweetest I ever saw on any face (unless perhaps a nun's when she has some grave kindness to do),"—and then I knew that my goal had been attained (*page* 32).

While the Humanistic type was being cut, Doctor Biagi came to America as the official representative from Italy to the St. Louis Exposition. Later, when he visited me in Boston, I took him to "Shady Hill" to see Mr. Norton. It was an historic meeting. The Italian had brought to America original, unpublished letters of Michelangelo, and at my suggestion he took them with him to Cambridge. Mr. Norton read several of these letters with the keenest interest and urged their publication, but Biagi was too heavily engaged with his manifold duties as librarian of the Laurenziana and Riccardi libraries, as custodian of the Buonarroti and the da Vinci archives, and with his extensive literary work, to keep the promise he made us that day.

The conversation naturally turned upon Dante, Biagi's rank in his own country as interpreter of the great poet being even greater than was Norton's in America. Beyond this they spoke of books, of art, of music, of history, of science. Norton's knowledge of Italy was profound and exact; Biagi had lived what Norton had acquired. No matter what the subject, their comments, although simply made, were expressions of prodigious study and absolute knowledge; of complete familiarity, such as one ordinarily has in every-day affairs, with subjects upon which even the well-educated man looks as reserved for profound discussion. Norton and Biagi were the two most cultured men I ever met. In listening to their conversation I discovered that a perfectly trained mind under absolute control is the most beautiful thing in the world.

Climbing the circular stairway in the old, ramshackle Harper plant at Franklin Square, New York, I used to find William Dean Howells in his sanctum.

"Take this chair," he said one day after a cordial greeting; "the only Easy Chair we have is in the *Magazine*."

Howells loved the smell of printer's ink. "They are forever talking about getting away from here," he would say, referring to the long desire at Harpers—at last gratified—to divorce the printing from the publishing and to move uptown.

183

"Here things are so mixed up that you can't tell whether you're a printer or a writer, and I like it."

Our acquaintance began after the publication by the Harpers in 1906 of a novel of mine entitled *The Spell*, the scene of which is laid in Florence. After reading it, Howells wrote asking me to look him up the next time I was in the Harper offices.

"We have three reasons to become friends," he said smiling, after studying me for a moment with eyes that seemed probably more piercing and intent then they really were: "you live in Boston, you love Italy, and you are a printer. Now we must make up for lost time."

After this introduction I made it a habit to "drop up" to his sanctum whenever I had occasion to go to Franklin Square to discuss printing or publishing problems with Major Leigh or Mr. Duneka. Howells always seemed to have time to discuss one of the three topics named in his original analysis, yet curiously enough it was rarely that any mention of books came into our conversation.

Of Boston and Cambridge he was always happily reminiscent: of entertaining Mr. and Mrs. John Hay while on their wedding journey, and later Bret Harte, in the small reception room in

120 West 57th St.,
May 6, 1917.

Dear Mr. Orcutt:

I think that if Mr. Burrows spoke my sister as one of his pupils she undoubtedly was so.

I have written some what of Jefferson in "My Literary Passions," and in an essay on "The Old Country Printer" in my volume of "Impressions and Experiences."

Yours sincerely,
W. D. Howells.

Autograph Letter from William Dean Howells

the Berkeley Street house, where the tiny "library" on the north side was without heat or sunlight when Howells wrote his *Venetian Days* there in 1870; of early visits with Mark Twain before the great fireplace in " the Cabin " at his Belmont home, over the door of which was inscribed the quotation from *The Merchant of Venice*, "From Venice as far as Belmont."—" In these words," Howells said, " lies the history of my married life ";—of the move from Belmont to Boston as his material resources increased.

"There was a time when people used to think I didn't like Boston," he would chuckle, evidently enjoying the recollections that came to him; "but I always loved it. The town did take itself seriously," he added a moment later; " but it had a right to. That was what made it Boston. Sometimes, when we know a place or a person through and through, the fine characteristics may be assumed, and we may chaff a little over the harmless foibles. That is what I did to Boston."

He chided me good-naturedly because I preferred Florence to Venice. " Italy," he quoted, "is the face of Europe, and Venice is the eye of Italy. But, after all, what difference does it make?" he asked. "We are both talking of the same wonderful country, and perhaps the intel-

186

lectual atmosphere of antiquity makes up for the glory of the Adriatic."

Then he told me a story which I afterwards heard Hamilton Mabie repeat at the seventy-fifth birthday anniversary banquet given Howells at Sherry's by Colonel George Harvey in 1912.

Two American women met in Florence on the Ponte Vecchio. One of them said to the other, "Please tell me whether this is Florence or Venice."

"What day of the week is it?" the other inquired.

"Wednesday."

"Then," said the second, looking at her itinerary, "this is Venice."

"I was born a printer, you know," Howells remarked during one of my visits. "I can remember the time when I couldn't write, but not the time when I couldn't set type."

He referred to his boyhood experiences in the printing office at Hamilton, Ohio. His father published there a Whig newspaper, which finally lost nearly all its subscribers because its publisher had the unhappy genius of always taking the unpopular side of every public question. Howells immortalized this printing office in his essay *The Country Printer*,—where he recalls "the compositors rhythmically swaying before their cases of type; the pressman flinging himself back on the bar that made the impression, with a swirl of his long hair; the apprentice rolling the forms; and the foreman bending over them."

The Lucullan banquet referred to outrivaled that given by Colonel Harvey to Mark Twain. How Mark Twain would have loved to be there, and how much the presence of this life-long friend would have meant to Howells! More than four hundred men and women prominent in letters gathered to do honor to the beloved author, and President Taft conveyed to him the gratitude of the nation for the hours of pleasure afforded by his writings.

In the course of his remarks, Howells said:

I knew Hawthorne and Emerson and Walt Whitman; I knew Longfellow and Holmes and Whittier and Lowell; I knew Bryant and Bancroft and Motley; I knew Harriet Beecher Stowe and Julia Ward Howe; I knew Artemus Ward and Stockton and Mark Twain; I knew Parkman and Fiske.

As I listened to this recapitulation of contact with modern humanists, I wondered what Howells had left to look forward to. No one could fail to envy him his memories, nor could he fail to ask himself what twentieth-century names would be

FRIENDS THROUGH THE PEN

written in place of those the nineteenth century
had recorded in the Hall of Fame

My library has taken on a different aspect during
all these years. When I first installed my books I
looked upon it as a sanctuary, into which I could
escape from the world outside. Each book was a
magic carpet which, at my bidding, transported
me from one country to another, from the present
back to centuries gone by, gratifying my slightest
whim in response to the mere effort of changing
volumes. My library has lost none of that blissful
peace as a retreat, but in addition it has become a
veritable meeting ground. The authors I have
known are always waiting for me there,—to
disclose to me through their works far
more than they, in all modesty, would
have admitted in our personal
conferences

CHAPTER VI
Triumphs of Typography

VI

TRIUMPHS OF TYPOGRAPHY

IN gathering together his book treasures, a collector naturally approaches the adventure from a personal standpoint. First editions may particularly appeal to him, or Americana, or his bibliomania may take the form of subject collecting. I once had a friend who concentrated on whales and bees! My hobby has been to acquire, so far as possible, volumes that represent the best workmanship of each epoch, and from them I have learned much of fascinating interest beyond the history of typography. A book in itself is always something more than paper and type and binder's boards. It possesses a subtle friendliness that sets it apart from other inanimate objects about us, and stamps it with an individuality which responds to our approach in proportion to our interest. But aside from its contents, a typographical monument is a barometer of civilization. If we discover what economic or political conditions combined to make it stand out from other products of its period, we learn contemporaneous history and become acquainted with the personalities of the people and the manners and customs of the times.

No two countries, since Gutenberg first discovered the power of individual types when joined together to form words down to the present day, have stood pre-eminent in the same epoch in the art of printing. The curve of supremacy, plotted from the brief triumph of Germany successively through Italy, France, the Netherlands, England, France, and back again to England, shows that the typographical monuments of the world are not accidental, but rather the natural results of cause and effect. In some instances, the production of fine books made the city of their origin the center of culture and brought luster to the country; in others, the great master-printers were attracted from one locality to another because of the literary atmosphere in a certain city, and by their labors added to the reputation it had already attained. The volumes themselves sometimes produced vitally significant effects; sometimes their production was the result of conditions equally important.

The first example I should like to own for my collection of typographical triumphs is, of course, the *Gutenberg Bible (opp. page)*; but with only forty-five copies known to be in existence (of

194

Part of a Page from the Mazarin Copy of the Gutenberg Bible, Mayence, 1455
Bibliothèque Nationale, Paris [Exact size]

which twelve are on vellum), I must content myself with photographic facsimile pages. The copy
most recently offered for sale brought $106,000
in New York in February, 1926, and was later
purchased by Mrs. Edward S. Harkness for
$120,000, who presented it to the Yale Univer-
sity Library. This makes the *Gutenberg Bible* the
most valuable printed book in the world,—six
times as precious as a Shakespeare first folio.
Fortunately, the copies are well distributed, so that
one need not deny himself the pleasure of studying
it. In America, there are two examples (one on
vellum) in the Pierpont Morgan Library, in New
York; another in the New York Public Library,
and still another in the library of the General
Theological School; while the private collections
of Henry E. Huntington and Joseph E. Widener
are also fortunate possessors. In England, one may
find a copy at the British Museum or the Bodleian
Library; on the Continent, at the Bibliothèque
Nationale at Paris, at the Vatican Library in
Rome, or in the libraries of Berlin, Leipzig,
Munich, or Vienna. Over twenty of the forty-
five copies are imperfect, and only four are still
in private hands. Of these four, one is imperfect,
and two are already promised to libraries; so the
copy sold in New York may be the last ever offered.

196

GUTENBERG BIBLE

And here is the end of the first part of the Bible, that is to say, the Old Testament, rubricated and bound for Henry Cremer, in the year of our Lord, one thousand four hundred and fifty-six, on the feast of the Apostle Bartholomew Thanks be to God. Alleluia

Rubricator's Mark at End of Second Volume of the Mazarin Copy in the Bibliothèque Nationale, Paris

GUTENBERG BIBLE

This book was illuminated, bound, and completed for Henry Cremer, Vicar of Saint Stephens of Mayence, in the year of our Lord, one thousand four hundred and fifty-six, on the feast of the Ascension of the Glorious Virgin Mary. Thanks be to God. Allehia

Rubricator's Mark at End of Fourth Volume of the Mazarin Copy in the Bibliothêque Nationale, Paris

The copy that I love best to pore over—always discovering something interesting that had previously escaped me,—is the daddy of them all, at the Bibliothèque Nationale at Paris. This is the one De Bure discovered in the library of Cardinal Mazarin in Paris in 1763,—three hundred years after it was printed, and until then unknown. It is bound in four massive volumes of red morocco, stamped with the arms of Louis XIV. At the end of the second volume (*page* 196), and again at the end of the fourth (*page* 197), are rubricator's notes, giving the date of the completion of the work as August 15, 1456. Think how important this is in placing this marvel of typography; for the project of printing the *Bible* could not have been undertaken earlier than August, 1451, when Gutenberg formed his partnership with Fust and Schoeffer in Mayence.

To a modern architect of books the obstacles which the printer at that time encountered, with the art itself but a few years old, seem insurmountable. There was the necessity of designing and cutting the first fonts of type, based upon the hand lettering of the period. As is always inevitable in the infancy of any art, this translation from one medium to another repeated rather than corrected the errors of the human hand. The typesetter,

ANNALES TYPOGRAPHICI
AB ARTIS INVENTÆ
ORIGINE .
AD ANNUM MD.
Opera
MICH. MAITTAIRE A.M.
Hagæ-Comitum.
Sumptibus Ifaaci Vaillant.

ı Joannes Gutemberg. ııı Laurentius Costerus. ıv Aldus Manucius.
ıı Joannes Fauſtus.   v Joannes Frobenius.

GUTENBERG, FUST, COSTER, ALDUS, FROBEN
From Engraving by Jacob Houbraken (1698-1780)

John Fuſt, from an Old Engraving

inſtead of being secured from an employment office, had to be made. Gutenberg himself, per-haps, had to teach the apprentice the method of joining together the various letters, in a roughly-made composing ſtick of his own invention, in such a way as to maintain regularity in the diſtances between the ſtems of the various letters, and thus produce a uniform and pleasing appearance. There exiſted no proper iron chases in which to lock up the pages of the type, so that while the metal could be made secure at the top and bottom, there are frequent inſtances where it bulges out on the sides.

From the very beginning the printed book had to be a work of art. The patronage of kings and princes had developed the hand-lettered volumes to the highest point of perfection, and, on account of this keen competition with the scribes and their patrons, no printer could afford to devote to any volume less than his utmost artistic taste and mechanical ingenuity. Thus today, if a reader examines the *Gutenberg Bible* with a critical eye, he will be amazed by the extraordinary evenness in the printing, and the surprisingly accurate align-ment of the letters. The glossy blackness of the ink still remains, and the sharpness of the im-pression is equal to that secured upon a modern cylinder press.

It has been estimated that no less than six hand presses were employed in printing the 641 leaves, composed in double column without numerals, catch words, or signatures. What binder today would undertake to collate such a volume in proper sequence! After the first two divisions had come off the press it was decided to change the original scheme of the pages from 40 to 42 lines. In order to get these two extra lines on the page it was necessary to set all the lines closer together. To accomplish this, some of the type was recast, with minimum shoulder, and the rest of it was actually cut down in height to such an extent that a portion of the curved dots of the *i*'s was clipped off.

TRIUMPHS OF TYPOGRAPHY

Monographs have been written to explain the variation in the size of the type used in different sections of this book, but what more natural explanation could there be than that the change was involuntary and due to natural causes? In those days the molds which the printer used for casting his types were made sometimes of lead, but more often of wood. As he kept pouring the molten metal into these matrices, the very heat would by degrees enlarge the mold itself, and thus produce lead type of slightly larger size. From time to time, also, the wooden matrices wore out, and the duplicates would not exactly correspond with those they replaced.

In printing these volumes, the precedent was established of leaving blank spaces for the initial letters, which were later filled in by hand. Some of these are plain and some elaborate, serving to make the resemblance to the hand-lettered book even more exact; but the glory of the *Gutenberg Bible* lies in its typography and presswork rather than in its illuminated letters.

Germany, in the *Gutenberg Bible,* proved its ability to produce volumes worthy of the invention itself, but as a country it possessed neither the scholars, the manuscripts, nor the patrons to insure the development of the new art. Italy, at the end of the fifteenth century, had become the home of learning, and almost immediately Venice became the Mecca of printers. Workmen who had served their apprenticeships in Germany sought out the country where princes might be expected to become patrons of the new art, where manu-scripts were available for copy, and where a public existed both able and willing to purchase the products of the press. The Venetian Republic, quick to appreciate this opportunity, offered its protection and encouragement. Venice itself was the natural market of the world for distribution of goods because of the low cost of sea transportation.

I have a fine copy of Augustinus: *De Civitate Dei* (*page* 205) that I discovered in Rome in its original binding years ago, printed in Jenson's Gothic type in 1475. On the first page of text, in bold letters across the top, the printer has placed the words, *Nicolaus Jenson, Gallicus.* In addition to this signature, the *explicit* reads:

This work De Civitate *is thus happily completed, being done in Venice by that excellent and diligent master, Nicolas Jenson, while Pietro Mochenicho was Doge, in the year after the birth of the Lord, one thousand four hundred and seventy-five, on the sixth day before the nones of October (2 October)*

Aurelij Auguſtini opus de ciuita
te dei feliciter explicit:confectuz uene
tijs ab egregio ꝛ diligēti magiſtꝛo Ni
colao ienſon:Petro moꝛenicho prin
cipe:Anno a natiuitate domini mile
ſimo quadringēteſimo ſeptuageſimo
quinto:ſexto nonas octobres.

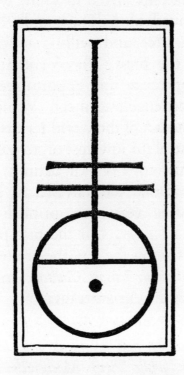

Nicolas Jenson's Explicit and Mark

Jenson was a printer who not only took pride in his art but also in the country of his birth! He was a Frenchman, who was sent to Mayence by King Charles VII of France to find out what sort of thing this new art of printing was, and if of value to France to learn it and to bring it home. Jenson had been an expert engraver, so was well adapted for this assignment. At Mayence he quickly mastered the art, and was prepared to transport it to Paris; but by this time Charles VII had died, and Jenson knew that Louis XI, the new monarch, would have little interest in recognizing his father's mandate. The Frenchman then set himself up in Venice, where he contributed largely to the prestige gained by this city as a center for printing as an art, and for scholarly publications.

Jenson had no monopoly on extolling himself in the *explicits* of his books. The cost of paper in those days was so high that a title page was considered an unnecessary extravagance, so this was the printer's only opportunity to record his imprint. In modern times we printers are more modest, and leave it to the publishers to sound our praises, but we do like to place our signatures on well-made books!

The *explicit* in the hand-written book also offered a favorite opportunity for gaining immortality for

N dicet aliquis ista falsa eē mi‚
raculaꞏnec fuisse facta sz mdaci
ter scripta ? Quisquis hoc dicitꞏsi de
his rebᵇ negat oio ull’ l̃ziis eē crededū:
pōt ēt dicē:nec õoꝶ ullos curaꞁ moꝛta‚
lia. Non enim se aliter colenos esse
persuaserunt:nisi mirablibus operuꞁ
effectibus:quoꝶ ꝛ hiſtoꝛia gentiuꞁ
teſtis eſt:quaꞁ dij se oſtentare mirabi
les:potius ꝗ utiles oñdere potueꝛt.
Uñ hoc opere nꝛo:cuius hunc iã deci
mum librum habemus in manibus:
ñ eos suscepimus refellenos:qui uel
ullā esse uim diuinam negant:uel hu‚
mana non curare contendūt:sz eos q̃
nꝛo deo conditoꝛi sancte ꝛ gloꝛiosiſſi‚
me ciuitatis deos suos preferūt:nesci‚
entes eum esse ipsum etiam mūdi hu‚
ius uisibilis ꝛ mutabilis inuisibilē ꝛ i‚
cōmutabilem conditoꝛem ꝛ uite bea‚
te:ñ de his que condidit:sed de seipso
ueriſſimum largitoꝛem. Eius enim p̃
pheta ueraciſſimus ait. Mihi autem
adherere deo bonum eſt. De fine nãꝗ
boni inter philosophos querit:ad q̃
adipiscendum omnia officia refereda
ſunt. Nec dixit iſte:mihi autem nimis
diuitijs abundare bonum eſt:aut insi
gniri purpura ꝛ sceptro: uel diadēate
excellere:aut quod nonnulli etiaꞁ phi
losophoꝶ dicē non erubuerunt:mihi
uoluptas coꝛpoꝛis bonum ē: aut q̃
melius uelut melioꝛes dicere uiſi ſūt:
mihi uirtus animi bonum eſt. Sz mi
hi inquit adherere deo bonū eſt. hoc
euꞁ õocuerat:cui uni tantūmõ sacri
ficandum:sancti quoꝗ angeli legaliū
sacrificioꝶ etiam conteſtatione mo
nuerunt. Uñ ēt ipse sacrificiū eius fact²
fuerat:cuius igne intelligibili cōꝛept²
ardebat:ꝛ in eius ineffabilem incoꝛpo
reūꝗ complexum sancto desiderio fc
rebatur. Poꝛꝛo autem ſi multoꝶ õo‚
rum cultoꝛes: qualescūꝗ deos suos
esse arbitrentur:ab eis facta esse mira
cula uel ciuilium rerum hiſtoꝛie:uel li

bris magicis:ſiue q̃õ honeſtius pu
tant theurgicis credunt:quid cause ē
cur illis litteris nolunt credere iſta fac
ta esse:quibus tãto maioꝛ debet fides
quanto sup oĩs eſt magnus: cui uni
soli sacrificandum precipiunt.

Que ratio ſit uiſibilis sacrificij: ꝗ
uni uero ꝛ inuiſibili deo offerri õocet
uera religio.cap.xix.

Q̃ui autem putant hec uiſibilia
sacrificia dijs aliꝗs congruere:il
li uero tãnquam inuiſibili inuiſibilia
ꝛ maioꝛa maioꝛi: melioꝛiꝗ meliora:
qualia ſunt pūre mentis ꝛ bone uolū
tatis officia:pꝛofecto nesciunt hec ita
esse ſigna illoruꞁ:ſicut uerba uel ſonã
tia ſigna ſunt rerum. Quocirca ſicut
orantes atꝗ laudantes ad eum dirigi
mus ſignificantes uoces:cui res ipsas
in coꝛde:quas ſignificamus offerim²:
ita sacrificantes non alteri uiſibile sa‚
crificium offerendum esse nouerimuſ:
ꝗ illi cuius in coꝛdibus noſtris inuiſi
bile sacrificium nosipsi esse debemus.
Tunc nobis fauent nobisꝗ congau‚
dent:atꝗ ad hoc ipsum nos pꝛo ſuis
uiribus adiuuant angeli quiꝗ uirtu‚
tesꝗ superioꝛes:ꝛ ipsa bonitate ac pie
tate potentioꝛes. Si aūt illis hec exhi
bere uoluerimus:non libenter accipi‚
unt. ꝛ cum ad homines ita mittuntur
ut coꝛum presentia sentiat̃ aptiſſime
uetant:ſunt de his exempla in l̃ziis sãc
tis. Putauerunt quidam deferenduꞁ
angeliſ honoꝛē uel aõoranõo uel sacri
ficanõo qui debetur deo:ꝛ coꝛum ſūt
admonitione pꝛohibiti:iuſſiꝗ ſūt hec
ei deferre:cui uni fas esse nouerunt.
Imitati ſūt angelos sanctos ēt sancti
hoies dei. Nam paulus ꝛ barnabas i
lycaonia facto quodam miraculo sa‚
nitatis putati ſunt dij : eisꝗ lycaonij
immolare uictimas uoluerunt: quod
a se humili pietate remouentes eis in

Jenson's Gothic Type. From Augustinus: De Civitate Dei, *Venice,* 1475
[Exact size]

the scribe. I once saw in an Italian monastery a manuscript volume containing some 600 pages, in which was recorded the fact that on such and such a day Brother So-and-So had completed the transcribing of the text; and inasmuch as he had been promised absolution, one sin for each letter, he thanked God that the sum total of the letters exceeded the sum total of his sins, even though by but a single unit!

Among Jenson's most important contributions were his type designs, based upon the best hand lettering of the day. Other designers had slavishly copied the hand-written letter, but Jenson, wise in his acquired knowledge, eliminated the variations and produced letters not as they appeared upon the hand-written page, but standardized to the design which the artist-scribe had in mind and which his hand failed accurately to reproduce. The Jenson Roman (*page* 22) and his Gothic (*page* 205) types have, through all these centuries, stood as the basic patterns of subsequent type designers.

Jenson died in 1480, and the foremost rival to his fame is Aldus Manutius, who came to Venice from Carpi and established himself there in 1494. I have often conjectured what would have happened had this Frenchman printed his volumes in

France and thus brought them into competition with the later product of the Aldine Press. The supremacy of Italy might have suffered,—but could Jenson have cut his types or printed his books in the France of the fifteenth century? As it was, the glories of the Aldi so closely followed Jenson's superb work that Italy's supreme position in the history of typography can never be challenged.

For his printer's mark Aldus adopted the famous combination of the Dolphin and Anchor, the dolphin signifying speed in execution and the anchor firmness in deliberation. As a slogan he used the words *Festina lente*, of which perhaps the most famous translation is that by Sir Thomas Browne, " Celerity contempered with Cunctation." Jenson's printer's mark (*page* 203), by the way, has suffered the indignity of being adopted as the trademark of a popular brand of biscuits!

The printing office of Aldus stood near the Church of Saint Augustus, in Venice. Here he instituted a complete revolution in the existing methods of publishing. The clumsy and costly folios and quartos, which had constituted the standard forms, were now replaced by crown octavo volumes, convenient both to the hand and to the purse.

"I have resolved," Aldus wrote in 1490, "to devote my life to the cause of scholarship. I have chosen, in place of a life of ease and freedom, an anxious and toilsome career. A man has higher responsibilities than the seeking of his own enjoyment; he should devote himself to honorable

Device of Aldus Manutius

labor. Living that is a mere existence can be left to men who are content to be animals. Cato compared human existence to iron. When nothing is done with it, it rusts; it is only through constant activity that polish or brilliancy is secured."

The weight of responsibility felt by Aldus in becoming a printer may be better appreciated when one realizes that this profession then included the duties of editor and publisher. The publisher of

GROLIER IN THE PRINTING OFFICE OF ALDUS
After Painting by François Flameng
Courtesy The Grolier Club, New York City

today accepts or declines manuscripts submitted by their authors, and the editing of such manu‑ scripts, if considered at all, is placed in the hands of his editorial department. Then the "copy" is turned over to the printer for manufacture. In the olden days the printer was obliged to search out his manuscripts, to supervise their editing— not from previously printed editions, but from copies transcribed by hand, frequently by careless scribes. Thus his reputation depended not only on his skill as a printer, but also upon his sagacity as a publisher, and his scholarship as shown in his text. In addition to all this, the printer had to create the demand for his product and arrange for its distribution because there were no estab‑ lished bookstores.

The great scheme that Aldus conceived was the publication of the Greek classics. Until then only four of the Greek authors, Æsop, Theocritus, Homer, and Isocrates, had been published in the original. Aldus gave to the world, for the first time in printed form, Aristotle, Plato, Thucydides, Xenophon, Herodotus, Aristophanes, Euripides, Sophocles, Demosthenes, Lysias, Æschines, Plu‑ tarch, and Pindar. Except for what Aldus did at this time, most of these texts would have been irrevocably lost to posterity.

IN QUEST OF THE PERFECT BOOK

When you next see Italic type you will be interested to know that it was first cut by Aldus,
said to be inspired by the thin, inclined, cursive
handwriting of Petrarch; when you admire the
beauty added to the page by the use of small
capitals, you should give Aldus credit for having
been the first to use this attractive form of typography. Even in that early day Aldus objected to
the inartistic, square ending of a chapter occupying
but a portion of the page, and devised all kinds
of type arrangements, half-diamond, goblet, and
bowl, to satisfy the eye.

To me, the most interesting book that Aldus
produced was the *Hypnerotomachia Poliphili*,—
"Poliphilo's Strife of Love in a Dream." It
stands as one of the most celebrated in the annals
of Venetian printing, being the only illustrated
volume issued by the Aldine Press. This work
was undertaken at the very close of the fifteenth
century at the expense of one Leonardo Crasso of
Verona, who dedicated the book to Guidobaldo,
Duke of Urbino. It was written by a Dominican
friar, Francesco Colonna, who adopted an ingenious method of arranging his chapters so that
the successive initial letters compose a complete
sentence which, when translated, read, "Brother
Francesco Colonna greatly loved Polia." Polia

POLIPHILO SEQVITA'NARRANDOOLTRATAN
TO CONVIVIO VNA ELEGANTISSIMA COREA CHE
FVE VNO GIOCO . ET COME LA REGINA AD DVE
PRAESTANTE PVERE SVE IL COMMISSE. LEQVALE
EL CONDVSERON ADMIRARE DELITIOSE ET MA-
GNE COSE, ET CONFABVLANDO ENVCLEATAMEN
TE LA MAESTRORONO COMMITANTE DALCVNE
DVBIETATE. FINALITER PERVENERON
AD LE TRE PORTE. ET COME ELLO
RIMANETE NELLA MEDIANA
PORTA, TRA LE AMORO-
SE NYMPHE.

TANTO EXCESSO ET INCOMPARABILE
gloria & triumphi, & inopinabile thesoro, & frugale de-
litie, & summe pompe, & solemne epulo, & lautissimo &
sumptuoso Symposio, di questa fœlicissima & opulen-
tissima Regina recensito, si io distincta & perfinitamen
te la sua præcipua dignitate non hauesse condignamen
te expresso, Nó se mirauegli dicio la curiosa turbula, Imperoche qualunque di acuto ingegno & expedito, & di prodiga & fertilissima lingua orna
to & copioso ad questo enucleata, ne coadunatamente potrebbe satisfare.
Ma molto meno io che continuamente patiua per qualunque intima la
tebra del mio inseruescente core, la indesinente pugna, quantúque absen
te di madona Polia, di omni mia uirtute occuparia & depopulabonda
prædatrice. De fora le molte mirauegle, di præcellentia inaudite di diuer
sitate, cose insuete & dissimile, inextimabile & non humane, Impero allu-
cinato & tutto æqualmente oppresso per omni mio senso, distracto per la
spectatissima uarietate la excessiua cótéplatiõe, di púcto in púncto io nó
lo saperei perfectamente descriuere, ne dignaméte propalare. Chiunque
cogitare ualeria il richo habito & exquisito ornato, & curiosissimo culto
la perfecta & ambitiosa & falerata bellecia sencia alcuno defecto, La sum-
ma sapientia, la Aemiliana eloquentia, La munificentia piu che regia.
La præclara dispositione di Architectura, & la obstinata Symmetria di
questo ædificio perfecta & absoluta, La nobilitate dellarte marmoraria.
La directione del columnamento, La perfectione distatue, Lornamen-
to di parieti, La uariatione di petre, Il uestibulo regale, amplissimo pe-
ristylio, Gli artificiosi pauimenti, Chi crederebbe di quanto luxo & im-

Text Page from Aldus' Hypnerotomachia Poliphili, *Venice, 1499 [11 x 7 inches].*
It is on this model that the type used in this volume is based

Hora quale animale che per la dolce esca, lo occulto dolo non perpen
de, postponendo el naturale bisogno, retro ad quella inhumana nota sen
cia mora cum uehementia festinante la uia, io andai. Alla quale quando
essere uenuto ragioneuolmente arbitraua, in altra parte la udiua, Oue &
quando a quello loco properante era giunto, altronde apparea essere affir
mata. Et cusi como gli lochi mutaua, similmente piu suaue & delecteuo-
le uoce mutaua cum cœlesti concenti. Dunque per questa inane fatica,
& tanto cum molesta sete corso hauendo, me debilitai tanto, che apena
poteua io el lasso corpo sustentare. Et gli affannati spiriti habili non essen
do el corpo grauemente affaticato hogi mai sostenire, si per el transacto pa
uore, si per la urgente sete, quale per el longo peruagabondo indagare,
& etiam per le graue anxietate, & per la calda hora, difeso, & relicto
dalle proprie uirtute, altro unquantulo desiderando ne appetendo, se
non ad le debilitate membra quieto riposo. Mirabondo dellaccidente
caso, stupido della melliflua uoce, & molto piu per ritrouarme in regio-
ne incognita & inculta, ma assai amœno paese. Oltra de questo, forte
me doleua, che el liquente fonte laboriosamente trouato, & cum tanto
solerte inquisito fusse sublato & perdito da gliochii mei. Per lequale tu-
te cose, io stetti cum lanimo intricato de ambiguitate, & molto trapen-
soso. Finalmente per tanta lassitudine correpto, tutto el corpo frigescen-

GROLIER BINDING
Castiglione: *Cortegiano*. Aldine Press, 1518
Laurenziana Library, Florence

has been identified as one Lucrezia Lelio, daughter of a jurisconsult of Treviso, who later entered a convent.

The volume displays a pretentious effort to get away from the commonplace. On every page Aldus expended his utmost ingenuity in the arrangement of the type,—the use of capitals and small capitals, and unusual type formations. In many cases the type balances the illustrations in such a way as to become a part of them. Based on the typographical standards of today, some of these experiments are indefensible, but in a volume issued in 1499 they stand as an extraordinary exhibit of what an artistic, ingenious printer can accomplish within the rigid limitations of metal type. The illustrations themselves, one hundred and fifty-eight in number, run from rigid architectural lines to fanciful portrayals of incidents in the story. Giovanni Bellini is supposed to have been the artist, but there is no absolute evidence to confirm this supposition.

Some years ago the Grolier Club of New York issued an etching entitled, *Grolier in the Printing Office of Aldus* (*page* 208). I wish I might believe that this great printer was fortunate enough to have possessed such an office! In spite of valuable concessions he received from the Republic, and the success accorded to him as a printer, he was able to eke out but a bare existence, and died a poor man. The etching, however, is important as emphasizing the close relation which existed between the famous ambassador of François I at the Court of Pope Clement VII, at Rome, and the family of Aldus, to which association booklovers owe an eternal debt of gratitude. At one time the Aldine Press was in danger of bankruptcy, and Grolier not only came to its rescue with his purse but also with his personal services. Without these tangible expressions of his innate love for the book, collectors today would be deprived of some of the most interesting examples of printing and binding that they count among their richest treasures.

The general conception that Jean Grolier was a binder is quite erroneous; he was as zealous a patron of the printed book as of the binder's art. His great intimacy in Venice was with Andrea Torresani (through whose efforts the Jenson and the Aldus offices were finally combined), and his two sons, Francesco and Federico, the father-in-law and brothers-in-law of the famous Aldus. No clearer idea can be gained of Grolier's relations at *Casa Aldo* than the splendid letter which he sent to Francesco in 1519, intrusting to his hands the making of Budé's book, *De Asse:*

GROLIER BINDING
Capella: *L'Anthropologia Digaleazzo*. Aldine Press, 1533
From which the Cover Design of this Volume was adapted
(Laurenziana Library, Florence. 7½ x 4¼ inches)

You will care with all diligence, he writes, O most beloved Francesco, that this work, when it leaves your printing shop to pass into the hands of learned men, may be as correct as it is possible to render it. I heartily beg and beseech this of you. The book, too, should be decent and elegant; and to this will contribute the choice of the paper, the excellence of the type, which should have been but little used, and the width of the margins. To speak more exactly, I should wish it were set up with the same type with which you printed your Poliziano. And if this decency and elegance shall increase your expenses, I will refund you entirely. Lastly, I should wish that nothing be added to the original or taken from it.

What better conception of a book, or of the responsibility to be assumed toward that book, both by the printer and by the publisher, could be expressed today!

The early sixteenth century marked a crisis in the world in which the book played a vital part. When Luther, at Wittenberg, burned the papal bull and started the Reformation, an overwhelming demand on the part of the people was created for information and instruction. For the first time the world realized that the printing press was a weapon placed in the hands of the masses for defence against oppression by Church or State.

François I was King of France; Charles V, Emperor of the Holy Roman Empire; and Henry VIII, King of England. Italy had something to think about beyond magnificently decorated volumes, and printing as an art was for the time forgotten in supplying the people with books at low cost.

François I, undismayed by the downfall of the Italian patrons, believed that he could gain for himself and for France the prestige which had been Italy's through the patronage of learning and culture. What a pity that he had not been King of France when Jenson returned from Mayence! He was confident that he could become the Mæcenas of the arts and the father of letters, and still control the insistence of the people, which increased steadily with their growing familiarity with their new-found weapon. He determined to have his own printer, and was eager to eclipse even the high standard the Italian master-printers had established.

Robert Étienne (or Stephens), who in 1540 succeeded Néobar as " Printer in Greek to the King," while not wholly accomplishing his monarch's ambitions, was the great master-printer of his age. He came from a family of printers, and received his education and inspiration largely from the

216

Robert Étienne
Scavant Imprimeur par sa parfaite
connoissance des langues et des belles lettres
né à Paris mort Protestant à Genève l'an 1559
age de   46 ans

Desrochers   Thib.

Ce Scavant à jamais vivra
Digne du Temple de Memoire:
Et chez les Imprimeurs sa gloire,
Autant que leur Art durera.   Thib.

ROBERT ÉTIENNE, 1503-1559
Royal Printer to François I
From Engraving by Étienne Johandier Desrochers (c. 1661-1741)

learned men who served as correctors in his father's office. François proved himself genuinely inter⁄ested in the productions of his *Imprimerie Royale*, frequently visiting Étienne at the Press, and en⁄couraging him by expending vast sums for specially designed types, particularly in Greek. The story goes that on one occasion the King found Étienne engaged in correcting a proof sheet, and refused to permit the printer to be disturbed, insisting on waiting until the work was completed.

For my own collection of great typographical monuments I would select for this period the *Royal Greeks* of Robert Étienne. A comparison between the text page, so exquisitely balanced (*page* 222), and the title page (*page* 220), where the arrangement of type and printer's mark could scarcely be worse, gives evidence enough that even the artist⁄printer of that time had not yet grasped the wonderful opportunity a title page offers for self⁄expression. Probably Étienne regarded it more as a chance to pay his sovereign the compliment of calling him "A wise king and a valiant warrior." But are not the Greek characters marvelously beautiful! They were rightly called the *Royal Greeks*! The drawings were made by the celebrated calligrapher Angelos Vergetios, of Candia, who was employed by François to make transcripts of Greek texts for the Royal Collection, and whose manuscript volumes may still be seen in the Bibliothèque Nationale in Paris. Earlier fonts had been based upon this same principle of making the Greek letters reproductions as closely as possible of the elaborate, involved, current writing hand of the day; but these new designs carried out the principle to a degree until then unattained. The real success of the undertaking was due to the skill of Claude Garamond, the famous French punchcutter and typefounder. Pierre Victoire quaintly comments:

Besides gathering from all quarters the remains of Hellenic literature, François I added another benefit, itself most valuable, to the adornment of this same honorable craft of printing; for he provided by the offer of large moneys for the making of extremely graceful letters, both of Greek and Latin. In this also he was fortunate, for they were so nimbly and so delicately devised that it can scarce be conceived that human wit may compass anything more dainty and exquisite; so that books printed from these types do not merely invite the reader,—they draw him, so to say, by an irresistible attraction.

Of course, they were too beautiful to be practical. In the Roman letters typecutters had already found that hand lettering could no more be translated

ΤΗΣ ΚΑΙΝΗΣ ΔΙΑΘΗΚΗΣ ΑΠΑΝΤΑ.

ΕΥΑΓΓΕΛΙΟΝ

Κατὰ Ματθαῖον.
Κατὰ Μάρκον.
Κατὰ Λουκᾶν.
Κατὰ Ἰωάννην.

ΠΡΑΞΕΙΣ ΤΩΝ ΑΠΟΣΤΟΛΩΝ.

Nouum IESV Christi D.N. Testamentum.

EX BIBLIOTHECA REGIA.

Βασιλεῖ τ᾽ ἀγαθῷ κρατερῷ τ᾽ αἰχμητῇ

LVTETIAE,

Ex officina Roberti Stephani typographi Regii, Regiis typis.

M. D. L.

ÉTIENNE'S *ROYAL GREEKS,* Paris, 1540
Title Page (10¼ x 6 inches)

directly into the form of type than a painting can be translated directly into a tapestry, without sacrificing some of the characteristic features of each. With the Greek letters, the problem was even more difficult, and the *Royal Greeks* offered no end of complications to the compositors, and added disastrously to the expense of the production. When Plantin came along, he based his Greek type upon Étienne's, but his modifications make it more practical. Compare the *Royal Greeks* with Plantin's Greek on page 231 and see how much beauty and variety was lost in the revision.

François I found himself in an impossible position between his desire to encourage Étienne in his publications and the terrific pressure brought to bear by the ecclesiastical censors. Just as the people had awakened to the value of books, not to put on shelves, but to read in order to know, so had the Church recognized the importance of controlling and influencing what those books contained. Throughout Robert Étienne's entire tenure of office there raged a conflict which not only seriously interfered with his work, but distinctly hampered the development of literature. Had François lived longer, Étienne's volumes might have reached a level equal to that attained by his Italian predecessors, but Henri II was no match

221

docent nomina illa, πηνελόπη, γραμμα-
τικὴ & ᾽ὀπιτομὴ, quæ Latinè à veteribus
per e reddita ſunt, Penelope, Gram-
matice, epitome.

DE TONIS, TEMPORI-
bus, ſpiritibus, & paſſionibus : quæ o-
mnia generali προςῳδίᾳν, id eſt accen-
tuū appellatione comprehenduntur.

Τόνοι, ſeu accétus ſunt tres. Acutus᾽
Ͽεός, λόγος, τύπῆο μῦν. Grauis ᾽ἱμὴ. Circunflexus ˜ ποιῶ, βοᾶτε. Acutus attollit
ſyllabá quam afficit: Grauis deprimit:
Circunflexus attollit atque deprimit.

Χρόνοι, id eſt Tempora duo, Lógum
& Breue : quorum prius hac nota - ſi-
gnificatur, & vocali productæ ſuperpo
nitur : Poſterius autem ita notatur ◡
vocalem correptam indicans.

Πνεύματα, hoc eſt Spiritus ſunt duo.
Aſper, ſiue denſus ᾽ ἅμα. Lenis, ſiue
tenuis ᾽ ἐγώ. Semper autē vocalis aut
diphthongus initio dictionis alterum

Page showing Étienne's Roman Face [Exact size]

ΤΟ ΚΑΤΑ ΜΑΤΘΑΙΟΝ ΑΓΙΟΝ
ΕΥΑΓΓΕΛΙΟΝ.

Ἰβλ@ γενέσεως ΙΗΣΟΥ χρι- **A**
ςοῦ, υἱοῦ Δαβὶδ, υἱοῦ Ἀβραάμ. Ἀ-
βραὰμ ἐγέννησε τὸν Ἰσαάκ. Ἰσαὰκ
δὲ ἐγέννησε τὸν Ἰακώβ. Ἰακὼβ δὲ ἐγέννησε τὸν Ἰούδαν κỳ τοὺς ἀδελφοὺς αὐτ̃.
Ἰούδας δὲ ἐγέννησε τῷ Φαρὲς καὶ τὸν
Ζαρὰ ἐκ τ̃ Θάμαρ. Φαρὲς ϳ̀ ἐγέννησε
τὸν Ἐσρώμ. Ἐσρὼμ δὲ ἐγέννησε τ̃ Ἀράμ. Ἀρὰμ δὲ ἐγέννησε
τ̃ Ἀμιναδάβ. Ἀμιναδὰβ δὲ ἐγέννησε τὸν Ναασσών. Ναασσὼν
ϳ̀ ἐγέννησε τὸν Σαλμών. Σαλμὼν δὲ ἐγέννησε τὸν Βοὸζ ἐκ τῆς
Ῥαχάβ. Βοὸζ ϳ̀ ἐγέννησε τὸν Ὠβὴδ ἐκ τ̃ Ῥὲθ. Ὠβὴδ ϳ̀ ἐγέν-
νησε τ̃ Ἰεσσαί. Ἰεσσαὶ δὲ ἐγέννησε τ̃ Δαβὶδ τὸν βασιλέα. Δαβὶδ ϳ̀ ὁ βασιλεὺς ἐγέννησε τὸν Σολομῶντα ἐκ τ̃ τ̃ Οὐρί. Σο-
λομῶν ϳ̀ ἐγέννησε τὸν Ῥοβοάμ. Ῥοβοὰμ δὲ ἐγέννησε τῷ Ἀ-
βιά. Ἀβιὰ ϳ̀ ἐγέννησε τὸν Ἀσά. Ἀσὰ ϳ̀ ἐγέννησε τ̃ Ἰωσαφάτ. **B**
Ἰωσαφὰτ ϳ̀ ἐγέννησε τ̃ Ἰωράμ. Ἰωρὰμ ϳ̀ ἐγέννησε τ̃ Ὀζίαν.
Ὀζίας ϳ̀ ἐγέννησε τὸν Ἰωάθαμ. Ἰωάθαμ ϳ̀ ἐγέννησε τὸν Ἄ-
χαζ. Ἄχαζ ϳ̀ ἐγέννησε τ̃ Ἐζεκίαν. Ἐζεκίας ϳ̀ ἐγέννησε τὸν Μα-
νασσῆ. Μανασσῆς ϳ̀ ἐγέννησε τὸν Ἀμών. Ἀμὼν ϳ̀ ἐγέννησε τὸν
Ἰωσίαν. Ἰωσίας ϳ̀ ἐγέννησε* τὸν Ἰεχονίαν ⟨ τοὺς ἀδελφοὺς αὐ-
τ̃, ἐπὶ τ̃ μετοικεσίας Βαβυλῶνος. μετ̃ ϳ̀ τὴν μετοικεσίαν Βαβυλῶνος, Ἰεχονίας ἐγέννησε τῷ Σαλαθιήλ. Σαλαθιὴλ δὲ
ἐγέννησε τὸν Ζοροβάβελ. Ζοροβάβελ δὲ ἐγέννησε τ̃ Ἀβιούδ.
Ἀβιοὺδ ϳ̀ ἐγέννησε τὸν Ἐλιακείμ. Ἐλιακεὶμ ϳ̀ ἐγέννησε τὸν Ἀ-
ζώρ. Ἀζὼρ δὲ ἐγέννησε τὸν Σαδώκ. Σαδὼκ ϳ̀ ἐγέννησε τὸν Ἀ-
χείμ. Ἀχεὶμ ϳ̀ ἐγέννησε τὸν Ἐλιούδ. Ἐλιοὺδ δὲ ἐγέννησε τὸν Ἐ-

a.i.

ÉTIENNE'S *ROYAL GREEKS*
Text Page (10¼ x 6 inches)
From *Novum Jesu Christi D. N. Testamentum*, Paris, 1540

Margin notes:
Λκ.γ.Ε
Γε.κβ.Δ. ἒ κι.Δ
Γε.κδ.Δ. ῃ λα.Η
α.Παρ.β.Α ρὺθ.δ.Δ
Ῥουθ.δ.Δ
α.Βασ.ις.Α ῃ ιζ.Β β.Βασ.ιβ.Ζ
α.Παρ.γ.Β
ς.Παρ.λς.Α δ.Βασ.κα.Δ α.παρ.γ.Γ δ.Βασ.κγ.Η ῃ κδ.Α β.παρ.λς.Β
α.Παρ.γ.Γ

for the censors. In 1552 Robert Étienne, worn out by the constant struggles, transferred his office to Geneva, where he died seven years later. His son Henri continued his work, but except for his *Thesaurus* produced little of typographical interest.

Had it not been for this bitter censorship, France might have held her supremacy for at least another half-century; but with the experiences of Robert Étienne still in mind, it is easily understood why the Frenchman, Christophe Plantin, in whom surged the determination to become a master-printer, sought to establish himself elsewhere.

By the middle of the sixteenth century Antwerp had assumed the proud position of leading city of Europe. The success that came to the Nether-landers in commerce as a result of their genius and enterprise later stimulated their interest in matters of religion, politics, and literature. Just as the tendencies of the times caused the pendulum to swing away from Italy to France, so now it swung from France toward the Netherlands. I had never before realized that, with the possible exception of certain communities in Italy, where the old in-tellectual atmosphere still obtained, there was no country in the world in which culture and intelligence were so generally diffused during the sixteenth century. How much more than typography these volumes have taught me!

It was inevitable that the art of printing should find in Belgium its natural opportunity for supreme expression. At the time Plantin turned his eyes in the direction of Antwerp, one entire quarter of that city was devoted to the manufacture of books. This apparently discouraged him, for at first he established himself as a bookbinder a little way out of the city. Later he added a shop for the sale of books; but in 1555 he moved boldly into Antwerp, becoming a full-fledged printer and publisher, soon demonstrating his right to recognition as the master-printer of his time.

By this time the words of Luther had attracted the attention of the Christian world more particularly than ever to the Bible. The people considered it the single basis of their faith, and upon their familiarity with it depended their present and future welfare. It was natural that they should attach the greatest importance to the possession of the most authentic edition of the original text. What more glorious task, then, could a printer take upon himself than to provide correct texts, to translate them with scrupulous exactitude, and to produce with the greatest perfection the single book upon which was based the welfare of men and of empires!

CHRISTOPHORVS PLANTINVS
TVRONENSIS   E. de Boulonois Sculp.

CHRISTOPHE PLANTIN, 1514-1589
From Engraving by Edme de Boulonois (c. 1550)

This was the inspiration that came to Chriſtophe Plantin, and which gradually took form in the *Biblia Polyglotta*, the great typographic achievement of the sixteenth century. On the left-hand page should appear the original Hebrew text, and in a parallel column should be a rendering into the Vulgate (*page* 230). On the right-hand page the Greek version would be printed, and beside it a Latin translation (*page* 231). At the foot of each page should be a Chaldean paraphrase.

Antwerp was then under Spanish domination. Plantin at once opened negotiations with Philip II of Spain, and was finally successful in securing from that monarch an agreement to subsidize the undertaking,—a promise which unfortunately was never kept. It is probable that the King was influenced toward a favorable decision by the ſtruggle that occurred between Frankfort, Heidel-berg, and even Paris, for the honor of being associated with the great work. Philip subscribed for thirteen copies upon parchment, and agreed to pay Plantin 21,200 florins. He ſtipulated, however, that the work should be executed under the personal supervision of one Arias Montanus, whom he would send over from Spain. Plantin accepted this condition with some misgivings, but upon his arrival Montanus captivated all by his personal charm and profound learning.

In February, 1565, Plantin employed Robert Grandjon, an engraver of Lyons, to cut the Greek characters for the work, basing his font upon the *Royal Greeks*. They are still beautiful because they are still unpractical, but they cannot compare with their models any more than later fonts of Greek, cut with the rigid requirements of typography in mind, can compare with these. Grandjon also supplied Plantin with all his Roman, and part of his Hebrew types, the balance being cut by Guillaume Le Bé, of Paris, Hautin of Rochelle, Van der Keere of Tours, and Corneille Bomberghe of Cologne.

The eight massive parts of the *Biblia Polyglotta* appeared during the years 1568 to 1573. The first volume opens with a splendid engraved title, representing the union of the people in the Christian faith, and the four languages of the Old Testament (*opp. page*). In the lower, right-hand corner appears the famous Plantin mark. Immediately following are two other engraved plates (*page 232*), illustrative as well as decorative in their nature. One of these pages gives to the faithless Philip an undeserved immortality. There are also single full-page engravings at the beginning of the fourth and fifth volumes. Twelve copies were printed on vellum for King Philip. A thir-

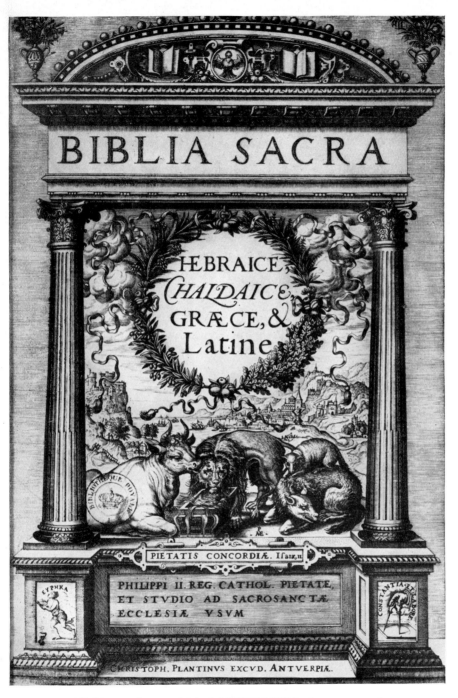

PLANTIN'S *BIBLIA POLYGLOTTA,* Antwerp, 1568
Title Page
(13¼ x 8¼ inches)

PRAEFATIO

nam bene confecti itineris gloria constet, imprimis cognoscere, exploratúmq. habere maximè conuenit. Verùm enim uero communis cuiusdam humanæ naturæ hostis & aduersarii infensissimi callida excogitatáque malitia & opera accidit, vt hæc tam propria & necessaria, quam indicauimus, in hominibus notitia perturbata fuerit; vt, postquam homo de proprio illustri & celso statu conuulsus, déque adiunctis vltra naturalem facultatem ex diuina gratia magnarum dotum præsidiis deiectus in eum locum, quem nunc tenet, miserè deuenit, si tantùm homo & nullo præterea maiori auxilio instructus, nullo superiori duce vsus, nulla maiori luce illustratus fuerit, quamuis multum cogitet, coniectet, atque exerceatur, nunquam tamen tantum cogitatione & notitia consequatur, vt maxima & copiosissima pars earum rerum quas cognouerit & explorauerit, cum minima earum, quas ignorat, portione conferri comparariq. possit (vt de aliarum etiam virtutum damno in illa prima ruina accepto nihil impræsentiarũ dicamus) ita vt post multum studium, multámque operam adhibitam, tamen in plurimis rebus atque rationibus, quas sibi notas exploratásque esse arbitretur, falli, labi, atque errare tandem deprehendatur. Quanquã enim humana mens veri inueniendi & cognoscendi auida & capax natura sua, atque adeò inuenti amantissima sit: quòd tamen ad illius inuentionem ratiocinatione plerunque vtatur; sæpenumero accidit ex permixta boni & mali, qua præditus est, cognitione, atq. ex communis aduersarii artibus & dolis, vt aut in ipso ratiocinandi vsu, vel malè explicandis initiis, vel perperã ineunda ratione, decipiatur. Aliquando enim falsa pro veris, incerta pro certis admittuntur, ex quibus nihil verum, nihílve certum deduci queat: & tametsi maximè certa atque explorata principia sint; tamen quòd cum propositi & quæsiti generis ratione non cohæreant, totam argumentationem labefactant. Quòd si hanc cognitionis primam lucem turbatam & obscuratam esse contingat, cæteram omnem actionem & vitæ hinc instituendæ viam vel peruersam, vel certè ancipitem, atque dubiam fore necesse

Hebrew column

רֵאשִׁית בָּרָא אֱלֹהִים אֵת הַשָּׁמַיִם וְאֵת
הָאָרֶץ: וְהָאָרֶץ הָיְתָה תֹהוּ וָבֹהוּ וְחֹשֶׁךְ
עַל־פְּנֵי תְהוֹם וְרוּחַ אֱלֹהִים מְרַחֶפֶת עַל־
פְּנֵי הַמָּיִם: וַיֹּאמֶר אֱלֹהִים יְהִי־אוֹר
וַיְהִי־אוֹר: וַיַּרְא אֱלֹהִים אֶת־הָאוֹר כִּי־טוֹב וַיַּבְדֵּל
אֱלֹהִים בֵּין הָאוֹר וּבֵין הַחֹשֶׁךְ: וַיִּקְרָא אֱלֹהִים לָאוֹר
יוֹם וְלַחֹשֶׁךְ קָרָא לָיְלָה וַיְהִי־עֶרֶב וַיְהִי־בֹקֶר יוֹם אֶחָד:
וַיֹּאמֶר אֱלֹהִים יְהִי רָקִיעַ בְּתוֹךְ הַמַּיִם וִיהִי כְּבֹדֵיל
בֵּין מַיִם לָמָיִם: וַיַּעַשׂ אֱלֹהִים אֶת־הָרָקִיעַ וַיַּבְדֵּל בֵּין
הַמַּיִם אֲשֶׁר מִתַּחַת לָרָקִיעַ וּבֵין הַמַּיִם אֲשֶׁר מֵעַל לָרָקִיעַ
וַיְהִי־כֵן: וַיִּקְרָא אֱלֹהִים לָרָקִיעַ שָׁמָיִם וַיְהִי־עֶרֶב
וַיְהִי־בֹקֶר יוֹם שֵׁנִי: וַיֹּאמֶר אֱלֹהִים יִקָּווּ הַמַּיִם
מִתַּחַת הַשָּׁמַיִם אֶל־מָקוֹם אֶחָד וְתֵרָאֶה הַיַּבָּשָׁה וַיְהִי־
כֵן: וַיִּקְרָא אֱלֹהִים לַיַּבָּשָׁה אֶרֶץ וּלְמִקְוֵה הַמַּיִם קָרָא
יַמִּים וַיַּרְא אֱלֹהִים כִּי־טוֹב: וַיֹּאמֶר אֱלֹהִים תַּדְשֵׁא
הָאָרֶץ דֶּשֶׁא עֵשֶׂב מַזְרִיעַ זֶרַע עֵץ פְּרִי עֹשֶׂה פְּרִי לְמִינוֹ
אֲשֶׁר זַרְעוֹ־בוֹ עַל־הָאָרֶץ וַיְהִי־כֵן: וַתּוֹצֵא הָאָרֶץ דֶּשֶׁא
עֵשֶׂב מַזְרִיעַ זֶרַע לְמִינֵהוּ וְעֵץ עֹשֶׂה־פְּרִי אֲשֶׁר זַרְעוֹ־בוֹ
לְמִינֵהוּ וַיַּרְא אֱלֹהִים כִּי־טוֹב: וַיְהִי־עֶרֶב וַיְהִי־בֹקֶר
יוֹם שְׁלִישִׁי: וַיֹּאמֶר אֱלֹהִים יְהִי מְאֹרֹת בִּרְקִיעַ
הַשָּׁמַיִם לְהַבְדִּיל בֵּין הַיּוֹם וּבֵין הַלָּיְלָה וְהָיוּ לְאֹתֹת
וּלְמוֹעֲדִים וּלְיָמִים וְשָׁנִים: וְהָיוּ לִמְאוֹרֹת בִּרְקִיעַ
הַשָּׁמַיִם לְהָאִיר עַל־הָאָרֶץ וַיְהִי־כֵן: וַיַּעַשׂ אֱלֹהִים
אֶת־שְׁנֵי הַמְּאֹרֹת הַגְּדֹלִים אֶת־הַמָּאוֹר הַגָּדֹל לְמֶמְשֶׁלֶת
הַיּוֹם וְאֶת־הַמָּאוֹר הַקָּטֹן לְמֶמְשֶׁלֶת הַלַּיְלָה וְאֵת
הַכּוֹכָבִים: וַיִּתֵּן אֹתָם אֱלֹהִים בִּרְקִיעַ הַשָּׁמַיִם לְהָאִיר
עַל־הָאָרֶץ: וְלִמְשֹׁל בַּיּוֹם וּבַלַּיְלָה וּלְהַבְדִּיל בֵּין הָאוֹר
וּבֵין הַחֹשֶׁךְ וַיַּרְא אֱלֹהִים כִּי־טוֹב: וַיְהִי־עֶרֶב וַיְהִי־
בֹקֶר יוֹם רְבִיעִי: וַיֹּאמֶר אֱלֹהִים יִשְׁרְצוּ הַמַּיִם שֶׁרֶץ
נֶפֶשׁ חַיָּה וְעוֹף יְעוֹפֵף עַל־הָאָרֶץ עַל־פְּנֵי רְקִיעַ הַשָּׁמַיִם

Latin column

CAPVT PRIMVM.

N principio creauit Deus cælum & terra. * Terra autem
erat inanis & vacua: & tenebræ erant super faciẽ abyssi:
& spiritus Dei ferebatur su-
per aquas. * Dixitq́, Deus, Fiat lux. Et facta est
lux. * Et vidit Deus lucem quòd esset bona:&
diuisit lucem à tenebris. * Appellauitq́; lucem
diem;& tenebras nocte. Factumq́; est vespere
& mane dies vnus. * Dixit quoque Deus, Fiat
firmamentũ in medio aquarum; & diuidat a-
quas ab aquis. * Et fecit Deus firmamentum,
diuisitq́; aquas quæ erant sub firmamento, ab
his quæ erant super firmamentũ. Et factum est
ita. * Vocauitq́, Deus firmamentũ,cælum: &
factum est vespere, & mane dies secundus.
* Dixit verò Deus, Congregentur aquæ quæ
sub cælo sunt, in locum vnum:& appareat ari-
da.Et factum est ita. * Et vocauit Deus aridã,
terram: congregationẽq́; aquarum appellauit
maria. Et vidit Deus quòd esset bonum. * Et
ait, Germinet terra herbã virentẽ & facientem semen; & lignum pomiferũ faciens fructũ
iuxta genus suum, cuius semen in semetipso sit
super terram.Et factũ est ita. * Et protulit terra
herbam virentẽ, & facientẽ semen iuxta genus
suũ;lignumq́; faciens fructũ, & habens vnum-
quodq́; sementem secundũ speciem suam. Et
vidit Deus quòd esset bonum. * Et factum est
vespere & mane dies tertius. * Dixit autẽ Deus,
Fiant luminaria in firmamento cæli ; & diuidant diem ac nocte; * & sint in signa & tẽpora
& dies & annos: * Vt luceãt in firmamẽto cæli,
& illuminent terrã.Et factum est ita. * Fecitq́;
Deus duo luminaria magna: luminare maius,
vt præesset dici:& luminare minus,vt præesset
nocti: & stellas. * Et posuit eas Deus in firmamẽto cæli,vt lucerẽt super terrã: * Et præessent
dici ac nocti;& diuiderent lucem ac tenebras.
* Et vidit Deus quòd esset bonũ. * Et factum est
vespere, & mane dies quartus. * Dixit etiam
Deus,Producantaquæ reptile animæ viuentis,
& volatile super terram sub firmamento cæli.

Marginal references: *Heb.11a*, *Psal.11*

תרגום אונקלוס

בְּקַדְמִין בְּרָא יְיָ יָת שְׁמַיָּא וְיָת אַרְעָא ² וְאַרְעָא הֲוָת צָדְיָא וְרֵיקָנְיָא וַחֲשׁוֹכָא עַל־אַפֵּי תְהוֹמָא וְרוּחָא דַיְיָ מְנַשְּׁבָא עַל
אַפֵּי מַיָּא: ³ וַאֲמַר יְיָ יְהֵא נְהוֹרָא וַהֲוָה נְהוֹרָא: ⁴ וַחֲזָא יְיָ יָת נְהוֹרָא אֲרֵי טָב וְאַפְרֵישׁ יְיָ בֵּין נְהוֹרָא וּבֵין
חֲשׁוֹכָא: ⁵ וּקְרָא יְיָ לִנְהוֹרָא יְמָמָא וְלַחֲשׁוֹכָא קְרָא לֵילְיָא וַהֲוָה רְמַשׁ וַהֲוָה צְפַר יוֹמָא חַד: ⁶ וַאֲמַר יְיָ יְהֵא רְקִיעָא בִּמְצִעוּת מַיָּא
וִיהֵא מַפְרֵישׁ בֵּין מַיָּא לְמַיָּא: ⁷ וַעֲבַד יְיָ יָת רְקִיעָא וְאַפְרֵישׁ בֵּין מַיָּא דְּמִלְרַע לִרְקִיעָא וּבֵין מַיָּא דְּמֵעַל לִרְקִיעָא וַהֲוָה כֵן: ⁸ וּקְרָא יְיָ
לִרְקִיעָא שְׁמַיָּא וַהֲוָה רְמַשׁ וַהֲוָה צְפַר יוֹם תִּנְיָן: ⁹ וַאֲמַר יְיָ יִתְכַּנְשׁוּן מַיָּא מִתְּחוֹת שְׁמַיָּא לַאֲתַר חַד וְתִתְחֲזֵי יַבֶּשְׁתָּא וַהֲוָה כֵן: ¹⁰ וּקְרָא
יְיָ לַיַּבֶּשְׁתָּא אַרְעָא וּלְבֵית כְּנִישׁוּת מַיָּא קְרָא יַמְמֵי וַחֲזָא יְיָ אֲרֵי טָב: ¹¹ וַאֲמַר יְיָ תַּדְאֵית אַרְעָא דִּתְאָה עִסְבָּא דְּבַר זַרְעֵיהּ מִזְדְּרַע אִילָן פֵּירִין עָבֵד
פֵּירִין לִזְנוֹהִי דְּבַר זַרְעֵיהּ בֵּיהּ עַל אַרְעָא וַהֲוָה כֵן: ¹² וְאַפֵּיקַת אַרְעָא דִּתְאָה עִסְבָּא דְּבַר זַרְעֵיהּ מִזְדְּרַע לִזְנוֹהִי וְאִילָן עָבֵד פֵּירִין דְּבַר זַרְעֵיהּ
בֵּיהּ לִזְנוֹהִי וַחֲזָא יְיָ אֲרֵי טָב: ¹³ וַהֲוָה רְמַשׁ וַהֲוָה צְפַר יוֹם תְּלִיתָאֵי: ¹⁴ וַאֲמַר יְיָ יְהוֹן נְהוֹרִין בִּרְקִיעָא דִּשְׁמַיָּא לְאַפְרָשָׁא בֵּין יְמָמָא
וּבֵין לֵילְיָא וִיהוֹן לְאָתִין וּלְזִמְנִין וּלְמִמְנֵי בְהוֹן יוֹמִין וּשְׁנִין: ¹⁵ וִיהוֹן לִנְהוֹרִין בִּרְקִיעָא דִּשְׁמַיָּא לְאַנְהָרָא עַל אַרְעָא וַהֲוָה כֵן: ¹⁶ וַעֲבַד יְיָ
יָת תְּרֵין נְהוֹרִין רַבְרְבַיָּא יָת נְהוֹרָא רַבָּא לְמִשְׁלַט בִּימָמָא וְיָת נְהוֹרָא זְעֵירָא לְמִשְׁלַט בְּלֵילְיָא וְיָת כּוֹכְבַיָּא: ¹⁷ וִיהַב יָתְהוֹן יְיָ בִּרְקִיעָא
דִּשְׁמַיָּא לְאַנְהָרָא עַל אַרְעָא: ¹⁸ וּלְמִשְׁלַט בִּימָמָא וּבְלֵילְיָא וּלְאַפְרָשָׁא בֵּין נְהוֹרָא וּבֵין חֲשׁוֹכָא וַחֲזָא יְיָ אֲרֵי טָב: ¹⁹ וַהֲוָה רְמַשׁ וַהֲוָה
צְפַר יוֹם רְבִיעָאֵי: ²⁰ וַאֲמַר יְיָ יְרַחֲשׁוּן מַיָּא רַחֲשָׁא נַפְשָׁא חַיְתָא וְעוֹפָא דְּפָרַח עַל אַרְעָא עַל אַפֵּי רְקִיעַ שְׁמַיָּא:

CAPVT PRIMVM.

IN principio fecit Deus cælum & terrá. At terra erat inuisibilis et incõposita, et tenebræ super abyssum: & spiritus Dei ferebatur su per aquam. Et dixit Deus, Fiat lux, & facta est lux. Et vidit Deus lucé, quòd bona: & diuisit Deus inter lucem, & inter tenebras. Et vocauit Deus lucé diè: & tenebras vocauit noctè: & factu est vespere; & factu est mane, dies vnus. Et dixit Deus, Fiat firmamentu in medio aquæ: & sit diuidés inter aquã, & aquã. Et fecit Deus firma mentu, & diuisit Deus inter aquã, quæ erat sub fir mameto: & inter aquã, quæ super firmamentu. Et vocauit Deus firmamentu cæli: & vidit Deus, quòd bonu. Et factu est vespere, & factu est mane, dies secũdus. Et dixit Deus, Cõgregetur aqua quæ sub cælo, in cõgregatione vnã, & appareat arida. Et factu est ita: & cõgregata est aqua quæ sub cælo, in cõgregatio ne suas: & apparuit arida. Et vocauit Deus aridã, terrã: & cõgregationes aquaru, vocauit maria. Et vi dit Deus quòd bonu. Et dixit Deus, Germinet terra herbã fœni seminante semé secundũ genus et secundũ similitudiné: & ligni pomiferu faciens fructu, cuius semen ipsi in ipso se.cundũ genus super terrã. Et fa ctum est ita. Et protulit terra herbã fœni seminante semen secundũ genus & secundũ similitudiné: & li gnũ pomiferu faciens fructu, cuius semé eius in ipso, secundũ genus super terrã. Et vidit Deus quòd bonu. Et factu est vespere, & factu est mane, dies ter tius. Et dixit Deus: Fiant luminaria in firmamento cæli, vt luceant super terrã, ad diuidendu inter diè, & inter noctè, & sint in signa, & in tēpora, & in dies, & in annos. Et sint in illuminationé in firma mento cæli, vt luceant super terram. Et factu est ita. Et fecit Deus duo luminaria magna: luminare ma gnu in principatus dici: & luminarè minus in prin cipatu noctis: et stellas. Et posuit eas Deus in firma mento cæli: vt luceret super terrã. Et præessent diei, & nocti: & diuiderét inter lucé et inter tenebras: et vidit Deus quòd bonu. Et factu est vespere, & factu est mane, dies quartus. Et dixit Deus, Producant a quæ reptilia animaru viuentiu, & volatilia volatia super terrã, secundũ firmamenti cæli: & factu est ita.

[Greek column]

ΕΝ ἀρχῇ ἐποίησεν ὁ θεὸς τὸν οὐρανὸν ἐ την γῆν. ἡ δὲ γῆ ἦν ἀόρατος ἐ ἀκατασκεύαστος, ἐ σκότος ἐπάνω τ̃ ἀβύσσου. ἐ πνεῦμα θεοῦ ἐπεφέ ρετο ἐπάνω τῦ ὕδατος. ἐ εἶπεν ὁ θεός, γυηθήτω φῶς. ἐ ἐγένετο φῶς. ἐ εἶδεν ὁ θεὸς τὸ φῶς, ὅτι καλόν. και διεχώρισεν ὁ θεὸς ἀναμέσον τῦ φωτός, ἐ ἀναμέσον τ̃ σκότους. ἐ ἐκάλεσεν ὁ θεὸς τὸ φῶς ἡμέραν, και τὸ σκότος ἐκά λεσε νύκτα. ἐ ἐγένετο ἑσπέρα, ἐ ἐγένετο πρωΐ, ἡμέρα μία. ἐ εἶ πεν ὁ θεός, γενηθήτω στερέωμα ἐν μέσω τῦ ὕδατος, ἐ ἔστω διαχωρίζον ἀναμέσον ὕδατος ἐ ὕδατος. ἐ ἐποίησεν ὁ θεὸς τὸ στερέωμα. ἐ διε χώρισεν ὁ θεὸς ἀναμέσον τῦ ὕδατος, ὃ ἦν ὑποκάτω τῦ στερεώματος, ἐ ἀναμέσον τῦ ὕδατος τῦ ἐπάνω τῦ στερεώματος. ἐ ἐκάλεσεν ὁ θεὸς τὸ στερέωμα οὐρανόν. ἐ εἶδεν ὁ θεὸς, ὅτι καλόν. ἐ ἐγένετο ἑσπέ ρα, ἐ ἐγένετο πρωΐ, ἡμέρα δευτέρα. καὶ εἶπεν ὁ θεός, συναχθήτω τὸ ὕδωρ τὸ ὑποκάτω τῦ οὐρανοῦ εἰς συναγωγὴν μίαν, ἐ ὀφθήτω ἡ ξηρά. καὶ ἐγένετο οὕτως. καὶ συνήχθη τὸ ὕδωρ τὸ ὑποκάτω τῦ οὐρανοῦ εἰς τὰς συναγωγὰς αὐτῶν, ἐ ὤφθη ἡ ξηρά. ἐ ἐκάλεσεν ὁ θεὸς τὴν ξηράν, γῆν. ἐ τὰ συστήματα τῶν ὑδάτων ἐκάλεσε θαλάσσας. ἐ εἶ δεν ὁ θεός, ὅτι καλόν. ἐ εἶπεν ὁ θεός, βλαστησάτω ἡ γῆ βοτάνην χόρτου σπεῖρον σπέρμα κατὰ γένος ἐ καθ' ὁμοιότητα, καὶ ξύλον κάρπιμον ποιοῦν καρπόν, οὗ τὸ σπέρμα αὐτοῦ ἐν αὐτῷ κατὰ γένος ἐπὶ τῆς γῆς. ἐ ἐγένετο οὕτως. καὶ ἐξήνεγκεν ἡ γῆ βοτάνην χόρτου σπεῖρον σπέρμα κατὰ γένος ἐ καθ' ὁμοιότητα, ἐ ξύλον κάρπι μον ποιοῦν καρπόν, οὗ τὸ σπέρμα αὐτοῦ ἐν αὐτῷ κατὰ γένος ἐπὶ τῆς γῆς. ἐ εἶδεν ὁ θεὸς ὅτι καλόν. καὶ ἐγένετο ἑσπέρα καὶ ἐγένε το πρωΐ, ἡμέρα τρίτη. ἐ εἶπεν ὁ θεός, γενηθήτωσαν φωστῆρες ἐν τῷ στερεώματι τῦ οὐρανοῦ εἰς φαῦσιν ἐπὶ τῆς γῆς, τῦ διαχωρίζειν ἀναμέσον τῦ ἡμέρας ἐ ἀναμέσον τῦ νυκτός, καὶ ἔστωσαν εἰς σημεῖα, καὶ εἰς καιρούς, καὶ εἰς ἡμέρας, καὶ εἰς ἐνιαυτούς. καὶ ἔστωσαν εἰς φαῦσιν ἐν τῷ στερεώματι τῦ οὐρανοῦ, ὥστε φαίνειν ἐπὶ τῆς γῆς. ἐ ἐγένετο οὕτως. ἐ ἐποίησεν ὁ θεὸς τοὺς δύο φωστῆρας τοὺς μεγάλους, τὸν φωστῆρα τὸν μέγαν εἰς ἀρχὰς τῆς ἡμέρας, καὶ τὸν φωστῆρα τὸν ἐλάσσω εἰς ἀρχὰς τῆς νυκτός, καὶ τοὺς ἀστέρας, καὶ ἔθετο αὐτοὺς ὁ θεὸς ἐν τῷ στερεώματι τῦ οὐρανοῦ, ὥστε φαίνειν ἐπὶ τῆς γῆς, ἐ ἄρχειν τῆς ἡμέρας καὶ τῆς νυκτός, καὶ διαχωρίζειν ἀναμέσον τῦ φω τὸς καὶ ἀναμέσον τῦ σκότους. καὶ εἶδεν ὁ θεὸς ὅτι καλόν. ἐ ἐγένε το ἑσπέρα καὶ ἐγένετο πρωΐ, ἡμέρα τετάρτη. ἐ εἶπεν ὁ θεός, ἐξα γαγέτω τὰ ὕδατα ἑρπετὰ ψυχῶν ζωσῶν, ἐ πετεινὰ πετόμενα ἐπὶ τῆς γῆς, κατὰ τὸ στερέωμα τῦ οὐρανοῦ. καὶ ἐγένετο οὕτως.

CHALDAICÆ PARAPHRASIS TRANSLATIO.
CAPVT PRIMVM.

IN principio creauit Deus cælum & terram. Terra autem erat deserta & vacua; & tenebræ super faciem abyssi: & spiritus Dei insufflabat super faciem aquarum. Et dixit Deus, Sit lux; & fuit lux. Et vidit Deus lucem quòd esset bona. Et diuisit Deus inter lucem & inter tenebras. Appellauitque Deus lucem diem, & tenebras vocauit noctem. Et fuit vespere & fuit mane dies vnus. Et dixit Deus, Sit firmamentum in medio aquarum: & diuidat inter aquas & aquas. Et fecit Deus firmamentum: & diuisit inter aquas quæ erant sub ter firmamento: & inter aquas quæ erant super firmamentum. Et fuit vespere & fuit mane, dies secundus. Et dixit Deus, Congregentur aquæ quæ sub cælo sunt, in locum vnum: & appareat arida. Et fuit ita. Et vocauit Deus aridam terram: & locum congregationis aquarum appellauit maria. Et vidit Deus quòd esset bonum. Et dixit Deus, Germinet terra germinationem herbæ, cuius filius sementis seminatur: arboremque fructiferam facientem fructus secundum genus suum; cuius filius sementis in ipso sit super terram. Et fuit ita. Et produxit terra germen herbæ, cuius filius sementis seminatur secundum genus suum; & arborem facientem fructus, cuius filius sementis in ipso secundum genus suum. Et vidit Deus quòd esset bonum. Et fuit vespere & fuit mane, dies tertius. Et dixit Deus, Sint luminaria in firmamento cæli, vt diuidant inter diem & noctem: & sint in signa & in tempora: & vt numerentur per ea dies & anni. Et sint in luminaria in firmamento cæli ad illuminandum super terram: & fuit ita. Et fecit Deus duo luminaria magna: lu minare maius, vt dominaretur in die: & luminare minus, vt dominaretur in nocte: & stellas. Et posuit eas Deus in firmamento cæli ad illuminan dum super terram. Et vt dominarentur in die & in nocte: & vt diuiderent inter lucem & tenebras: & vidit Deus quòd esset bonum. Et fuit vespere & fuit mane, dies quartus. Et dixit Deus, Serpant aquæ reptile animæ viuetis: & auem quæ volat super terrã super faciem aëris firmamenti cælorum.

A 2

PLANTIN'S *BIBLIA POLYGLOTTA*, Antwerp, 1568
Second Page
(13¼ x 8¼ inches)

teenth copy on vellum was never completed. In addition to these, ten other copies were printed on large Italian imperial paper, and were sold at 200 florins per copy. There were 300 copies on imperial paper at 100 florins, and 960 printed on fine royal Troyes paper, which were offered to the public at 70 florins each, with ten florins discount to libraries. One of the vellum copies was presented by the King to the Pope, another to the Duke of Alba, and still a third to the Duke of Savoy, the remaining copies being left in the library of the Escurial.

King Philip was so pleased with the volumes that he created Plantin *Prototypographe*, ruler over all the printers in the city,—a polite and inexpensive way of escaping his obligations. The world acclaimed a new master-printer; but these honors meant little to pressing creditors.

What a series of misfortunes Plantin endured! Stabbed by a miscreant who mistook him for some one else; hampered by censorship in spite of previous assurances of liberty in publications; his property wiped out again and again by the clashes of arms which finally cost Antwerp her pre-eminence; forever in debt, and having to sell his books below cost, and to sacrifice his library to meet pressing financial obligations;—yet always rising

233

above his calamities, he carried on his printing office until his death in 1589, when he left a comfortable fortune at above $200,000.

Historically, Plantin's contribution to the art of printing can scarcely be overestimated, yet technically he should be included in the second rather than the first group of early master-printers. The century that had elapsed since Gutenberg had removed many of the mechanical difficulties which had been obstacles to his predecessors. The printer could now secure printed copy to be edited and improved. Scholars were easily obtainable from the universities for editing and proofreading. Printing machinery could be purchased instead of being manufactured from original models. The sale of books had been greatly systematized. A printer could now devote himself to his art without dividing himself into various semi-related parts. Plantin proved himself a business man. Who else ever established a printing or publishing business on such an enduring basis that it continued for three hundred years! In bequeathing it to his daughter and his son-in-law, Moretus, Plantin made the interesting injunction that the printing office was always to be maintained by the son or successor who was most competent to manage it. If no son qualified, then the successor must be selected outside the family. Fortunately, however, there were sons who, each in his generation but with diminishing ability, proved his right to assume the responsibility, and the business was actually continued in the family down to 1867. A few years later the property was purchased by the city of Antwerp for 1,200,000 francs, and turned into a public museum.

I never visit the Plantin Museum at Antwerp without feeling that I have come closer to the old master-printers and their ideals. Here is the only great printing establishment of the past that time and the inroads of man have left intact. The beauty of the building, the harmony of the surroundings, the old portraits, the comfort yet the taste shown in the living-rooms,—all show that the artist-printer sought the same elements in his life that he expressed in his work. Entering from the Marché du Vendredi, I find myself face to face with a small tablet over the door on which is the device of Christophe Plantin, "first printer to the King, and the king of printers." Here the familiar hand, grasping a pair of compasses, reaches down from the clouds, holding the compasses so that one leg stands at rest while the other describes a circle, enclosing the legend *Labore et Constantia*. Within the house one finds the actual

235

types, and presses, and designs by Rubens and other famous artists, that were employed in making

Device of Christophe Plantin

the Plantin books. The rooms in which the master-printer lived make his personality very real. In those days a man's business was his life, and the home and the workshop were not far separated. Here the family life and the making of books were so closely interwoven that the visitor can scarcely tell where one leaves off and the other begins.

In the vocabulary of booklovers, the name *Elzevir* suggests something particularly choice and unique in the making of books. These volumes cannot compare favorably with many products of the press which preceded and followed them, yet the prestige which attended their publication has endured down to the present day. The original popularity of the Elzevirs was due to the fact that after a century of degradation, some one at last undertook to reclaim printing from the depths.

Printing, after reaching such heights so soon after its beginnings, had steadily declined. The art may really be said to have had its origin in Italy, as the work from Gutenberg's office, while extra-ordinary and epoch-making, could not rank with the best of the fifteenth-century Italian productions. The French volumes of the early sixteenth century were splendid examples of typography and press-work, but they did not equal those of their Italian predecessors. Christophe Plantin's work in Ant-werp was typographically unimportant except for his *Biblia Polyglotta*; and after Plantin, which takes us to the end of the sixteenth century, printing passed from an art into a trade. The Elzevirs were craftsmen rather than artists, but the best craftsmen of their period.

All this was a natural reaction. The book-buying public had come to demand the contents of the book at a cheaper price rather than volumes of greater technical excellence at a correspondingly higher cost. As we have seen, Sweynheim and Pannartz had ruined themselves by their experiments in Greek; the Aldine Press was saved from bankruptcy only by the intervention of Grolier. Henri Étienne, son of the great Robert Étienne, who endeavored to emulate his father's splendid work, came to financial grief in producing his *Thesaurus*; and Plantin could not have withstood the strain of his *Biblia Polyglotta* had it not been that he was commercially far-sighted enough to turn his plant over to the manufacture of inexpensive and less carefully made books.

By the end of the sixteenth century cheaper paper, made in Switzerland, came into the market, and this inferior, unbleached product largely replaced the soft, fine paper of Italian and French manufacture which had contributed in no small part to the beauty of the printed pages. Ink manufacturers had learned how to produce cheaper and poorer

238

ink, and the types themselves, through constant use, had become worn down to such an extent that real excellence was impossible.

Holland was the natural successor to Belgium in the supremacy of printing. The devastations of war had brought trade to a standstill in the Netherlands, while the city of Leyden had won the attention and admiration of the world for its heroic resistance during the long Spanish siege. To commemorate this event, William of Orange, in 1575, founded the University of Leyden, which quickly took high rank among scholars, and became the intellectual and literary center of Europe.

Thither the battle-scarred Plantin betook himself at the suggestion of Lipsius, the historian, who was now a professor in the new University. In Leyden, Plantin established a branch printing office. He was made Printer to the University, and for a time expected to remain here, but the old man could not bring himself to voluntary exile from his beloved Antwerp. Plantin's Leyden printing office had been placed in charge of Louis Elzevir, and when the veteran printer determined to return to Antwerp it would have seemed natural for him to leave it in Louis Elzevir's hands instead of turning it over to his son-in-law, Raphelengius.

239

This Elzevir, however, although the founder of the great Elzevir house, was not a practical printer, being more interested in bookselling and pub‑lishing; so distinction in printing did not come to the family until Isaac, Louis Elzevir's grandson, became Printer to the University in 1620. Fifteen years later, Bonaventura and Abraham Elzevir made the name famous through their editions of *Terence, Cæsar,* and *Pliny.*

Up to this time the favorite *format* had been the quarto volume, running about 12 by 18 inches in size. The Elzevirs boldly departed from the beaten path, and produced volumes running as small as 2 by 4 inches. They cut types of small size, show‑ing no special originality but based on good Italian models, and issued editions which at first met with small favor. "The Elzevirs are certainly great typographers," the scholar Deput wrote to Heinsius in 1629. "I can but think, however, that their reputation will suffer in connection with these trifling little volumes with such slender type."

Contrary to this prediction, the new *format* gradually gained favor, and finally became firmly established. The best publisher‑printers in France and Italy copied the Elzevir model, and the folios and the quartos of the preceding ages went en‑tirely out of style.

VENVS AFRA   SCIPIO AFR

PVB.
TERENTII
COMŒDIÆ
SEX
Ex recensione
Heinsiana.

Cornel. Cl. Dusend Sculpsit.

LVGD. BATAVORVM,
Ex Officina Elzeviriana. A.º 1635.

ELZEVIR'S *TERENCE,* 1635
Engraved Title Page [Exact size]

ELZEVIR'S *TERENCE*, Leyden, 1635
Text Pages [4 x 2 inches]

TRIUMPHS OF TYPOGRAPHY

The *Terence* of 1635 is the volume I selected for my collection (*page 242*). While not really beautiful, it is a charming little book. The copper-plate title (*page 241*) serves not only its original purpose but is also an illustration. The Elzevirs were wise enough to go back a hundred years and revive the practice of the copper-plate title, which had been discarded by intermediate printers because of its expense. The types themselves, far superior to other fonts in use at that time by other printers, were especially designed for the Elzevirs by Christoffel van Dyck. The interspacing of the capitals and the small capitals, the arrangement of the margins, and the general layout all show taste and knowledge of typographical precedent. The presswork would appear to better advantage except for the impossibility of securing ink of consistent quality.

The Elzevirs showed a great advance in business organization over any of their predecessors. Freed from oppressive censorship, they were able to issue a long list of volumes which were disposed of through connections established in the principal book centers of Italy, France, Germany, and Scandinavia, as well as throughout the Netherlands themselves. There is no record of any Elzevir publication proving a failure; but, by the same

token, one cannot say that the Elzevirs accomplished as much for the art to which they devoted
themselves as did the master-printers in whose
steps they followed.

Curiously enough, it was not until the eighteenth
century that England produced volumes which
were pre-eminent in any period. Caxton's work,
extraordinary as it was, competed against books
made at the same time in Venice by Jenson, and
were not equal to these Italian masterpieces. I
have a leaf from a Caxton volume which I often
place beside my Jenson volume, and the comparison always increases my wonder and admiration
for the great Italian printer. Caxton's work was
epoch-making, but until John Baskerville issued
his *Virgil* in Birmingham, in 1757, England had
not produced a volume that stood out, at the
moment of its publication, as the best of its time.
John Baskerville is one of the most unique
characters to be found in the annals of printing.
He had been in turn a footman, a writing teacher,
an engraver of slate gravestones, and the proprie-
tor of a successful japanning establishment. He
showed no special interest in types or books until
middle age, and after he had amassed a fortune.
Then, suddenly, he designed and cut types which

John Baskerville

(1706-1775)

competed successfully with the famous Caslon fonts, and produced his *Virgil*, which, as Benjamin Franklin wrote in presenting a copy to the Harvard College Library, was "thought to be the most curiously printed of any book hitherto done in the world." Macaulay called it, "The first of those magnificent editions which went forth to astonish all the librarians of Europe."

The Baskerville types were at first received with scant praise, although even the severest critics admitted that the Italic characters, from which was eliminated that cramped design seen in the Italics of other foundries of the period, were essentially beautiful. A letter written by Benjamin Franklin to Baskerville in 1760 is of amusing interest:

Let me give you a pleasant instance of the prejudice some have entertained against your work. Soon after I returned, discoursing with a gentleman concerning the artists of Birmingham, he said you would be the means of blinding all the readers of the nation, for the strokes of your letters being too thin and narrow, hurt the eye, and he could never read a line of them without pain. "I thought," said I, "you were going to complain of the gloss on the paper some object to." "No, no," said he, "I have heard that mentioned, but it is not that; it is in the form and cut of the letters themselves, they have not that height and thickness of the stroke which

245

makes the common printing so much more comfortable to the eye." You see this gentleman was a connoisseur. In vain I endeavored to support your character against the charge; he knew what he felt, and could see the reason of it, and several other gentlemen among his friends had made the same observation, etc.

Yesterday he called to visit me, when, mischievously bent to try his judgment, I stepped into my closet, tore off the top of Mr. Caslon's Specimen, and produced it to him as yours, brought with me from Birmingham, saying, I had been examining it, since he spoke to me, and could not for my life perceive the disproportion he mentioned, desiring him to point it out to me. He readily undertook it, and went over the several founts, showing me everywhere what he thought instances of that disproportion; and declared, that he could not then read the specimen without feeling very strongly the pain he had mentioned to me. I spared him that time the confusion of being told, that these were the types he had been reading all his life, with so much ease to his eyes; the types his adored Newton is printed with, on which he has pored not a little; nay, the very types his own book is printed with (for he is himself an author), and yet never discovered the painful disproportion in them, till he thought they were yours.

The *Virgil* itself, beyond the interest that exists in its type, shows grace and dignity in its composi-

PUBLII VIRGILII

MARONIS

BUCOLICA,

GEORGICA,

ET

AENEIS.

BIRMINGHAMIAE:

Typis JOHANNIS BASKERVILLE.

MDCCLVII.

Title Page of Baskerville's Virgil, Birmingham, 1757 [8½ x 5⅜ inches]

P. VIRGILII MARONIS

BUCOLICA

ECLOGA I. cui nomen *TITYRUS*.

MELIBOEUS, TITYRUS.

Tityre, tu patulæ recubans fub tegmine fagi
Silveftrem tenui Mufam meditaris avena:
Nos patriæ fines, et dulcia linquimus arva;
Nos patriam fugimus: tu, Tityre, lentus in umbra
5 Formofam refonare doces Amaryllida filvas.

   T. O Meliboee, Deus nobis hæc otia fecit:
Namque erit ille mihi femper Deus: illius aram
Sæpe tener noftris ab ovilibus imbuet agnus.
Ille meas errare boves, ut cernis, et ipfum
10 Ludere, quæ vellem, calamo permifit agrefti.

   M. Non equidem invideo; miror magis: undique totis
Ufque adeo turbatur agris. en ipfe capellas
Protenus æger ago: hanc etiam vix, Tityre, duco:
Hic inter denfas corylos modo namque gemellos,
15 Spem gregis, ah! filice in nuda connixa reliquit.
Sæpe malum hoc nobis, fi mens non læva fuiffet,
De coelo tactas memini prædicere quercus:
Sæpe finiftra cava prædixit ab ilice cornix.
Sed tamen, ifte Deus qui fit, da, Tityre, nobis.

20   *T.* Urbem, quam dicunt Romam, Meliboee, putavi
Stultus ego huic noftræ fimilem, quo fæpe folemus
Paftores ovium teneros depellere foetus.
Sic canibus catulos fimiles, fic matribus hoedos

A   Noram;

tion and margins. For the first time we have a type title (*page 247*) that shows a printer's appreciation of its possibilities. Baskerville affected extreme simplicity, employing no head or tail pieces and no ornamental initials to accomplish his effects (*page 249*).

The copy of Baskerville's *Virgil* in my library contains a copperplate frontispiece. The advertisement which particularly emphasized this feature excited my curiosity, as no book of Baskerville's is known to have contained illustrations. When I secured the copy I found that the frontispiece was a steel engraving stamped on water-marked paper which indicated its age to be at least two hundred years earlier than the publication of the book. The owner of this particular copy had inserted the illustration in re-binding, and it was no part of the original edition!

The glossy paper referred to in Franklin's letter was an outcome of Baskerville's earlier business experience. It occurred to him that type would print better upon highly finished paper, and that this finish could be secured by pressing the regular book paper of the time between heated japan plates made at his own establishment. Baskerville is entitled to the credit of having been the first printer to use highly finished paper, and, beyond this, as Dibdin says of him, "He united, in a singularly happy manner, the elegance of Plantin with the clearness of the Elzevirs."

Interest in the Baskerville books, and in fact in all books printed in what is known as "old-style" type, ceased suddenly with the inexplicable popularity attained about 1800 by the so-called "modern" face. The characteristics of the old-style letter are heavy ascending and descending strokes with small serifs, whereas the modern face accentuates the difference between the light and the heavy lines, and has more angular serifs. The engraved work of Thomas Bewick, in England, the publication of the *Racine* by the Didots, and the Bodoni volumes in Italy, offered the public an absolute innovation from the types with which they had been familiar since the invention of printing, and the new designs leaped into such popular favor that many of the foundries destroyed the matrices of their old-style faces, believing that the call for them had forever disappeared. As a matter of fact, it was not until the London publisher Pickering revived the old-style letter in 1844, that the modern face had any competition. Since then the two styles have been maintained side by side.

Thus the second supremacy of France came from a change in public taste rather than from economic causes. For a time there was a question whether Bodoni would win the distinction for Italy or the Didots for France, but the French printers pos-sessed a typographical background that Bodoni lacked, and in their *Racine* produced a master-piece which surpasses any production from the Bodoni Press. The Didots were not only printers and publishers, but manufactured paper and in-vented the process of stereotyping. While Min-ister to France, in 1780, Benjamin Franklin visited the Didot establishment, and, seizing the handle of a press, struck off several copies of a form with such professional familiarity as to cause astonishment.

"Don't be surprised," Franklin exclaimed smiling. "This, you know, is my real business."

In 1797, the French Minister of the Interior placed at the disposal of Pierre Didot *l'ainé* that portion of the Louvre which had formerly been occupied by the *Imprimerie Royale*. Here was be-gun, and completed in 1801, an edition of *Racine* in three volumes that aroused the enthusiasm of booklovers all over the world, and brought to Pierre Didot the glory of being recognized as a master-printer worthy to assume the mantle of

DIDOT'S *RACINE*, Paris, 1801
A Frontispiece
Designed by Prud'hon.   Engraved by Marius (12 x 8 inches)

OEUVRES

DE

JEAN RACINE.

. . . .

TOME PREMIER.

À PARIS,

DE L'IMPRIMERIE DE PIERRE DIDOT L'AÎNÉ,

AU PALAIS NATIONAL DES SCIENCES ET ARTS.

AN IX; M. DCCCI.

Title Page of Didot's Racine, Paris, 1801 [12 x 8 inches]

LA THÉBAÏDE,

OU

LES FRERES ENNEMIS,

TRAGÉDIE.

ACTE PREMIER.

SCENE I.

JOCASTE, OLYMPE.

JOCASTE.

Ils sont sortis, Olympe? Ah! mortelles douleurs!
Qu'un moment de repos me va coûter de pleurs!
Mes yeux depuis six mois étoient ouverts aux larmes,
Et le sommeil les ferme en de telles alarmes!
Puisse plutôt la mort les fermer pour jamaïs,
Et m'empêcher de voir le plus noir des forfaits!
Mais en sont-ils aux mains?

OLYMPE.

Du haut de la muraille
Je les ai vus déja tous rángés en bataille;
J'ai vu déja le fer briller de toutes parts;
Et pour vous avertir j'ai quitté les remparts.
J'ai vu, le fer en main, Étéocle lui-même;
Il marche des premiers; et, d'une ardeur extrême,
Il montre aux plus hardis a braver le danger.

JOCASTE.

N'en doutons plus, Olympe, ils se vont égorger.
Que l'on coure avertir et hâter la princesse;
Je l'attends. Juste ciel, soutenez ma foiblesse!
Il faut courir, Olympe, après ces inhumains;
Il les faut séparer, ou mourir par leurs mains.

Nous voici donc, hélas! a ce jour détestable
Dont la seule frayeur me rendoit misérable!
Ni prieres ni pleurs ne m'ont de rien servi;
Et le courroux du sort vouloit être assouvi.

Ó toi, Soleil, ô toi qui rends le jour au monde,
Que ne l'as-tu laissé dans une nuit profonde!
À de si noirs forfaits prêtes-tu tes rayons?
Et peux-tu sans horreur voir ce que nous voyons?
Mais ces monstres, hélas! ne t'épouvantent gueres;
La race de Laïus les a rendus vulgaires;
Tu peux voir sans frayeur les crimes de mes fils,

Page of Text, from Didot's Racine, Paris, 1801 [12 x 8 inches]

FIRMIN DIDOT, 1730-1804
From Engraving by Pierre Gustave Eugene Staal (1817-1882)

Robert Étienne. This is the typographic achievement I would select as the masterpiece of its period.

The large quarto volumes contain nearly five
hundred pages each. The type was designed and
cut by Firmin Didot in conjunction with, or
possibly in collaboration with Giambattista Bodoni, of Parma, Italy. So closely do the two faces
match that the similarity of their design could
scarcely have been a coincidence (see *page* 81).
There is a peculiar charm in the unusual length of
the ascending and descending characters; there is
a grace in the slender capitals in spite of the ultra-
refinement; there is satisfaction in having the weight
of the Italic letter approach that of the Roman, thus
preventing the usual blemish which the lighter
faced Italic gives to an otherwise perfectly balanced
page. The figures, really a cross between the old
style and the modern, have a distinct individuality
entirely lost in the so-called "lining" figures which
those who have copied this face in America have
introduced as an "improvement."

The *Racine* contains magnificent steel engravings, of which one is reproduced at page 253.
The handmade paper is a return to the beautiful
sheets of the fifteenth century, and the presswork—
the type just biting into the paper without leaving
an impression on the reverse side—is superbly

characteristic of the best French workmanship. The vellum copies show the work at its best. The engravings stand out almost as original etchings. The ink is the densest black I ever saw. Didot succeeded in overcoming the oil in the vellum without the chalk surface that is given to the Morris vellum, the ink being so heavy that it is slightly raised. I was particularly interested in this after my own experiments in printing my humanistic *Petrarch* on vellum.

At the Exposition of 1801, in Paris, the *Racine* was proclaimed by a French jury the "most perfect typographic product of any country and of any age." Is this not too high praise? To have equaled the Italian masterpieces of the fifteenth century would have been enough glory for any printer to claim!

The *Racine* was a step in the direction of reclaiming typography from the trade which it had become, but it was left for William Morris to place printing squarely back among the arts.

Morris was nearly sixty years of age when he finally settled upon the book as the medium through which to express his message to the world. The Morris wall papers, the Morris chair, the Morris end papers, are among his earlier experi-

WILLIAM MORRIS, 1834-1896
From Portrait by G. F. Watts, R. A. Painted in 1880
National Portrait Gallery, London

ments, all sufficiently unique to perpetuate his name; yet his work as a printer is what gave him undying glory. The *Kelmscott Chaucer* is his masterpiece, and must be included whenever great typographic monuments are named. For this the decorator-printer cut a smaller size of his Gothic font, secured the co-operation of Sir Edward Burne-Jones as illustrator, and set himself the task of designing the initial letters, borders, and decorations. This was in 1892, and for four years they worked upon it, one delay following another to make Morris fearful that the work might never be completed.

The decoration for the first page was finished in March, 1893. Morris was entirely satisfied with it, exclaiming, "My eyes! how good it is!" Then he laid the whole project aside for over a year, while he devoted himself to his metrical version of *Beowulf*. In the meantime Burne-Jones was experiencing great difficulty in having his designs satisfactorily translated onto wood, and Morris dolefully remarked, after comparing notes with his friend and collaborator, "We shall be twenty years at this rate in getting it out!"

It was June, 1894, before the great work was fairly under way. "*Chaucer* getting on well," Morris notes in his diary,—"such lovely designs."

At the end of June he records his expectation of beginning the actual printing within a month, and that in about three months more all the pictures and nearly all the borders would be ready for the whole of the Canterbury Tales.

About this time Morris was asked if he would accept the poet-laureateship of England, made vacant by Tennyson's death, if offered to him, and he unhesitatingly declined. His health and strength were noticeably failing, yet at the beginning of 1895, less than two years before his death, he was completely submerged by multifarious occupations. Two presses were running upon the *Chaucer* and still a third upon smaller books. He was designing new paper hangings and writing new romances; he was collaborating in the translation of *Heimskringla* and was supervising its production for the Saga Library; he was engaged in getting together his splendid collection of thirteenth- and fourteenth-century illuminated manuscripts.

It was not all smooth sailing with the *Chaucer*. In 1895 Morris discovered that many of the sheets had become discolored by some unfortunate ingredient of the ink, but to his immense relief he succeeded in removing the yellow stains by bleaching. "The check of the *Chaucer*," he writes,

SIR EDWARD BURNE-JONES, *Bart.,* 1833-1898
From Photograph at the British Museum

"flattens life for me somewhat, but I am going hard into the matter, and in about a fortnight hope to know the worst of it."

In December the *Chaucer* was sufficiently near completion to encourage him to design a binding for it. Even here he found another difficulty. "Leather is not good now," he complained; "what used to take nine months to cure is now done in three. They used to say 'What's longest in the tanyard stays least time in the market,' but that no longer holds good. People don't know how to buy now; they'll take anything."

Morris' anxiety over the *Chaucer* increased as it came nearer to completion. " I'd like it finished tomorrow!" he exclaimed. "Every day beyond tomorrow that it isn't done is one too many." To a visitor, looking through the printed sheets in his library, who remarked upon the added beauty of those sheets that follow the Canterbury Tales, where the picture pages face one another in pairs, Morris exclaimed in alarm, "Now don't you go saying that to Burne-Jones or he'll be wanting to do the first part over again; and the worst of that would be that he'd want to do all the rest over again because the other would be so much better, and then we should never get done, but be always going round and round in a circle."

The daily progress of the work upon the *Chaucer* was the one interest that sustained his waning energies. The last three blocks were brought to him on March 21, 1896. The Easter holidays almost killed him. "Four mouldy Sundays in a mouldy row," he writes in his diary. "The press shut and *Chaucer* at a standstill."

On May 6 all the picture sheets were printed and the block for the title page was submitted for Morris' approval, the final printing being completed two days later. On June 2 the first two bound copies were delivered to him, one of which he immediately sent to Burne-Jones, the other he placed in his own library.

Thus the *Kelmscott Chaucer* came to completion. William Morris died fourteen months later. The *Chaucer* had been nearly five years in preparation and three and a half years in execution. The printing alone had consumed a year and nine months. The volumes contain, besides eighty-seven illustrations by Burne-Jones, a full-page woodcut title, fourteen large borders, eighteen frames for pictures, and twenty-six large initial words, all designed by Morris, together with the smaller initials and the design for binding, which was in white pigskin with silver clasps, executed by Douglas Cockerell.

WICH torment, and with shameful   My throte is kut unto my nekke-boon,

Text Page of Kelmscott Chaucer, London, 1896 [15 x 10½ inches]

TRIUMPHS OF TYPOGRAPHY

I have never felt that the Kelmscott volumes were books at all, but were, rather, supreme examples of a master-decorator's taste and skill. After all, a book is made to read, and the *Kelmscott Chaucer* is made to be looked at. The principles which should control the design of the ideal book as laid down by William Morris cannot be improved upon, but when he undertook to put them into execution he found himself so wholly under the control of his decorating tendencies that he departed far from his text. William Morris' work is far greater than is shown in the volumes he printed. He awoke throughout the world an interest in printing as an art beyond what any other man has ever accomplished, the results of which have been a vital factor in bringing modern bookmaking to its present high estate.

It remained for T. J. Cobden-Sanderson, Morris' friend, admirer, and disciple, to put Morris' principles into operation at the Doves Press, London, supplemented by Emery Walker, who designed the Doves type,—to me the most beautiful type face in existence. Cobden-Sanderson, undisturbed by counter interests, plodded along, producing volumes into which he translated Morris' ideals far more consistently than did Morris himself. " The

Book Beautiful," Cobden-Sanderson wrote in his little masterpiece, *The Ideal Book,* "is a composite thing made up of many parts and may be made beautiful by the beauty of each of its parts—its literary content, its material or materials, its writing or printing, its illumination or illustration, its binding and decoration—of each of its parts in subordination to the whole which collectively they constitute; or it may be made beautiful by the supreme beauty of one or more of its parts, all the other parts subordinating or even effacing themselves for the sake of this one or more, and each in turn being capable of playing this supreme part and each in its own peculiar and characteristic way. On the other hand each contributory craft may usurp the functions of the rest and of the whole, and growing beautiful beyond all bounds ruin for its own the common cause."

The *Doves Bible* is Cobden-Sanderson's masterpiece, and one turns to it with relief after the riotous beauty of the Morris pages. It is printed throughout in one size of type with no leads between the lines and with no paragraphs, the divisions being indicated by heavy paragraph marks. The only decorative feature of any description consists of exceedingly graceful initial letters at the beginning of each new book. The

THE ENGLISH BIBLE

CONTAINING THE OLD TESTAMENT & THE NEW TRANS
LATED OUT OF THE ORIGINAL TONGUES BY SPECIAL COM
MAND OF HIS MAJESTY KING JAMES THE FIRST AND NOW
REPRINTED WITH THE TEXT REVISED BY A COLLATION OF
ITS EARLY AND OTHER PRINCIPAL EDITIONS AND EDITED
BY THE LATE REV. F. H. SCRIVENER M.A. LL.D. FOR THE
SYNDICS OF THE UNIVERSITY PRESS CAMBRIDGE

VOL. V

THE NEW TESTAMENT

THE DOVES PRESS
Nº I THE TERRACE HAMMERSMITH
MDCCCCV

Title Page of Doves Bible, *London,* 1905 *[8 x 6 inches]*

THE GOSPEL ACCORDING TO S. JOHN

IN the beginning was the Word, and the Word was with God, and the Word was God. The same was in the beginning with God. All things were made by him; and without him was not any thing made that was made. In him was life; and the life was the light of men. And the light shineth in darkness; and the darkness comprehended it not. ❡ There was a man sent from God, whose name was John. The same came for a witness, to bear witness of the Light, that all men through him might believe. He was not that Light, but was sent to bear witness of that Light. That was the true Light, which lighteth every man that cometh into the world. He was in the world, & the world was made by him, & the world knew him not. He came unto his own, and his own received him not. But as many as received him, to them gave he power to become the sons of God, even to them that believe on his name: which were born, not of blood, nor of the will of the flesh, nor of the will of man, but of God. And the Word was made flesh, & dwelt among us, (and we beheld his glory, the glory as of the only begotten of the Father,) full of grace and truth. John bare witness of him, and cried, saying, This was he of whom I spake, He that cometh after me is preferred before me: for he was before me. And of his fulness have all we received, & grace for grace. For the law was given by Moses, but grace and truth came by Jesus Christ. No man hath seen God at any time; the only begotten Son, which is in the bosom of the Father, he hath declared him. ❡ And this is the record of John, when the Jews sent priests and Levites from Jerusalem to ask him, Who art thou? And he confessed, & denied not; but confessed, I am not the Christ. And they asked him, What then? Art thou Elias? And he saith, I am not. Art thou that prophet? And he answered, No. Then said they unto him, Who art thou? that we may give an answer to them that sent us. What sayest thou of thyself? He said, I am the voice of one crying in the wilderness, Make straight the way of the Lord, as said the prophet Esaias. And they which were sent were of the Pharisees. And they asked him, & said unto him, Why baptizest thou then, if thou be not that Christ, nor Elias, neither that prophet? John answered them, saying, I baptize with water: but there standeth one among you, whom ye know not; he it is, who coming after me is preferred before me, whose shoe's latchet I am not worthy to unloose. These things were done in Bethabara beyond Jordan, where John was baptizing. ❡ The next day John seeth Jesus coming unto him, and saith, Behold the Lamb of God, which taketh away the sin of the world. This is he of whom I said, After me cometh a man which is preferred before me: for he was before me. And I knew him not: but that he should be made manifest to Israel, therefore am I come baptizing with water. And John bare record, saying, I saw the Spirit descending from heaven like a dove, and it abode upon him. And I knew him not: but he that sent me to baptize with water, the same said unto me, Upon whom thou shalt see the

Text Page of Doves Bible, *London,* 1905 *[8 x 6 inches]*

type is based flatly upon Jenson's Roman face, and exactly answers Morris' definition of the type ideal, " Pure in form, severe, without needless excrescences, solid without the thickening and thinning of the lines, and not compressed laterally." The presswork is superb.

Surely no form of bibliomania can yield greater rewards in return for study and perseverance. The great typographical monuments, dating from 1456 to 1905, have given me a composite picture of man's successful struggle to free himself from the bonds of ignorance. I have mingled with Lorenzo the Magnificent and with the oppressed people of Florence; I have been a part of François I's sumptuous Court, and have seen the anxious faces of the clerical faction as they read the writing on the wall; I have listened to the preaching of Luther, and have heard the Spanish guns bombarding Antwerp; I have stood with the brave defenders of Leyden, and have watched the center of learning find its place in Holland; I have enjoyed Ben Franklin's participation in the typographical efforts of Baskerville and Didot; I have received the inspiration of seeing William Morris and Cobden-Sanderson put a great art back into its rightful place. These triumphs of the printing

TRIUMPHS OF TYPOGRAPHY

press are far more than books. They stand as landmarks charting the path of culture and learning
through four marvelous centuries
What volume of the twentieth century and what
master-printer shall be included? That is yet to
be determined by the test of retrospect; but the
choice will be more difficult to make. In
America and England history is being
made in printing as an art, and
the results are full of hopeful
ness and promise

CHAPTER VII
The Spell of the Laurenziana

VII

THE SPELL OF THE LAURENZIANA

THE most fascinating city in all Europe is Florence, and the most alluring spot in all Florence is the Laurenziana Library. They say that there is something in the peculiar atmosphere of antiquity that reacts curiously upon the Anglo-Saxon temperament, producing an obsession so definite as to cause indifference to all except the magic lure of culture and learning. This is not difficult to believe after working, as I have, for weeks at a time, in a cell-like alcove of the Laurenziana; for such work, amid such surroundings, possesses an indescribable lure.

Yet my first approach to the Laurenziana was a bitter disappointment; for the bleak, unfinished façade is almost repelling. Perhaps it was more of a shock because I came upon it directly from the sheer beauty of the Baptistery and Giotto's Campanile. Michelangelo planned to make this façade the loveliest of all in Florence, built of marble and broken by many niches, in each of which was to stand the figure of a saint. The plans, drawn before America was discovered, still exist, yet work has never even been begun. The façade remains unfinished, without a window and unbroken save by three uninviting doors.

Conquering my dread of disillusionment, I approached the nearest entrance, which happened to be that at the extreme right of the building and led me directly into the old Church of San Lorenzo. Drawing aside the heavy crimson curtains, I passed at once into a calm, majestic quiet and peace which made the past seem very near. I drew back into the shadow of a great pillar in order to gain my poise. How completely the twentieth century turned back to the fifteenth! On either side, were the bronze pulpits from which Savonarola thundered against the tyranny and intrigue of the Medici. I seemed to see the militant figure standing there, his eyes flashing, his voice vibrating as he proclaimed his indifference to the penalty he well knew he drew upon himself by exhorting his hearers to oppose the machinations of the powerful family within whose precincts he stood. Then, what a contrast! The masses vanished, and I seemed to be witnessing the gorgeous beauty of a Medici marriage procession. Alessandro de' Medici was standing beneath a *baldacchino*, surrounded by the pomp and glory of all

274

Florence, to espouse the daughter of Charles V. Again the scene changes and the colors fade. I leave my place of vantage and join the reverent throng surrounding the casket which contains the mortal remains of Michelangelo, and listen with bowed head to Varchi's eloquent tribute to the great humanist.

The spell was on me! Walking down the nave, I turned to the left and found myself in the Old Sacristy. Verrocchio's beautiful sarcophagus in bronze and porphyry recalled for a moment the personalities and deeds of Piero and Giovanni de' Medici. Then on, into the "New" Sacristy, —new, yet built four centuries ago! Again I paused, this time before Michelangelo's tomb for Lorenzo the Magnificent, from which arise those marvelous monuments, "Day and Night" and "Dawn and Twilight,"—the masterpieces of a super-sculptor to perpetuate the memory of a super-man!

A few steps more took me to the Martelli Chapel, and, opening an inconspicuous door, I passed out into the cloister. It was a relief for the moment to breathe the soft air and to find myself in the presence of nature after the tenseness that came from standing before such masterpieces of man. Maurice Hewlett had prepared me for the "great, mildewed cloister with a covered-in walk all around it, built on arches. In the middle a green garth with cypresses and yews dotted about; when you look up, the blue sky cut square and the hot tiles of a huge dome staring up into it."

From the cloister I climbed an ancient stone staircase and found myself at the foot of one of the most famous stairways in the world. At that moment I did not stop to realize how famous it was, for my mind had turned again on books, and I was intent on reaching the Library itself. At the top of the stairway I paused for a moment at the entrance to the great hall, the *Sala di Michelangiolo*. At last I was face to face with the Laurenziana!

Before I had completed my general survey of the room, an attendant greeted me courteously, and when I presented my letter of introduction to the librarian he bowed low and led me the length of the hall. The light came into the room through beautiful stained-glass windows, bearing the Medici arms and the cipher of Giulio de' Medici, later Pope Clement VII, surrounded by arabesque Renaissance designs. We passed between the *plutei*, those famous carved reading-desks designed by Michelangelo. As we walked down the aisle, the pattern of the nutwood ceiling seemed reflected on the brick floor, so cleverly was the design repro-

276

SALA DI MICHELANGIOLO
Laurenziana Library, Florence

duced in painted bricks. Gradually I became impressed by the immense size of the room, which before I had not felt because the proportions are so perfect.

Doctor Guido Biagi, who was at that time librarian, was seated at one of the *plutei,* studying a Medicean illuminated manuscript fastened to the desk by one of the famous old chains (see *page* 14). He was a Tuscan of medium height, rather heavily built, with full beard, high forehead, and kindly, alert eyes. The combination of his musical Italian voice, his eyes, and his appealing smile, made me feel at home at once. Letters of introduction such as mine were every-day affairs with him, and no doubt he expected, as did I, to have our meeting result in a few additional courtesies beyond what the tourist usually receives, and then that each would go his way. I little realized, as I presented my letter, that this meeting was to be so significant,—that the man whose hand I clasped was to become my closest friend, and that through him the Laurenziana Library was to be for me a sanctuary.

After the first words of greeting, I said,

"I am wondering how much more I can absorb today. By mistake I came in through the church, and found myself confronted by a series

277

of masterpieces so overpowering that I am almost exhausted by the monuments of great personages and the important events they recall."

"A fortunate mistake," he replied smiling. "The entrance to the Library should be forever closed, and every one forced to come in through the church as you did, in order to absorb the old-world atmosphere, and be ready to receive what I can give.—So this is your first visit? You know nothing of the history of the Library?"

"Simply that everything was designed by Michelangelo,—and the names of some of the priceless manuscripts in your collection."

"It is not quite exact to say that everything was designed by the great Buonarroti," he corrected. "It was Michelangelo who conceived, but Vasari who designed and executed. Let me show you the letter the great artist wrote to Vasari about the stairway you just ascended" (*page* 280).

Leaving me for a moment he returned with a manuscript in his hand which he read aloud:

There is a certain stair that comes into my thoughts like a dream, the letter ran; but I don't think it is exactly the one which I had planned at the time, seeing that it appears to be but a clumsy affair. I will describe it for you here, nevertheless. I took a number of oval boxes,

278

Dott. Comm. GUIDO BIAGI in 1924
Librarian of the Laurenziana Library, Florence

each about one palm deep, but not of equal length and breadth. The first and largest I placed on a pavement at such distance from the wall of the door as seemed to be required by the greater or lesser degree of steepness you may wish to give the stair. Over this was placed another, smaller in all directions, and leaving sufficient room on that beneath for the foot to rest on in ascending, thus diminishing each step as it gradually retires towards the door; the uppermost step being of the exact width required for the door itself. This part of the oval steps must have two wings, one right and one left, the steps of the wings to rise by similar degree, but not be oval in form.

"Who but a great artist could visualize that marvelous staircase through a collection of wooden boxes!" Biagi exclaimed. "Vasari built this great room, but the designs were truly Michel-angelo's,—even to the carving of these *plutei*," he added, laying his hand on the reading-desk from which he had just risen. "See these chains, which have held these volumes in captivity for over four hundred years."

He asked me how long I was to be in Florence.

"For a week," I answered, believing the state-ment to be truthful; but the seven days stretched out into many weeks before I was able to break the chains which held me to the Library as firmly as if they were the links which for so many years

279

had kept the Medicean treasures in their hallowed places.

"Return tomorrow," he said. "Enter by the private door, where Marinelli will admit you. I want to keep your mind wholly on the Library."

The private door was the entrance in the portico overlooking the cloister, held sacred to the librarian and his friends. At the appointed hour I was admitted, and Marinelli conducted me immediately to the little office set apart for the use of the librarian.

"Before I exhibit my children," he said, "I must tell you the romantic story of this collection. You will enjoy and understand the books themselves better if I give you the proper background."

Here is the story he told me. I wish you might have heard the words spoken in the musical Tuscan voice:

Four members of the immortal Medici family contributed to the greatness of the Laurenziana Library, their interest in which would seem to be a curious paradox. Cosimo *il Vecchio*, father of his country, was the founder. " Old " Cosimo was unique in combining zeal for learning and an interest in arts and letters with political corruption. As his private fortune increased through success in trade he discovered the power money

280

VESTIBULE of the LAURENZIANA LIBRARY, FLORENCE
Designed by Michelangelo

possessed when employed to secure political prestige. By expending hundreds of thousands of
florins upon public works, he gave employment
to artisans, and gained a popularity for his family
with the lower classes which was of the utmost
importance at critical times. Beneath this guise of
benefactor existed all the characteristics of the
tyrant and despot, but through his money he was
able to maintain his position as a Mæcenas while
his agents acted as catspaws in accomplishing his
political ambitions. Old Cosimo acknowledged
to Pope Eugenius that much of his wealth had
been ill-gotten, and begged him to indicate a
proper method of restitution. The Pope advised
him to spend 10,000 florins on the Convent of
San Marco. To be sure that he followed this
advice thoroughly, Cosimo contributed more than
40,000 florins, and established the basis of the
present Laurenziana Library.

"Some of your American philanthropists must
have read the private history of Old Cosimo,"
Biagi remarked slyly at this point.

Lorenzo the Magnificent was Old Cosimo's
grandson, and his contribution to the Library was
far beyond what his father, Piero, had given.
Lorenzo was but twenty-two years of age when
Piero died, in 1469. He inherited no business

ability from his grandfather, but far surpassed him in the use he made of literary patronage. Lorenzo had no idea of relinquishing control of the Medici tyranny, but he was clever enough to avoid the outward appearance of the despot. Throughout his life he combined a real love of arts and letters with a cleverness in political manipulation, and it is sometimes difficult correctly to attribute the purpose behind his seeming benevolences. He employed agents to travel over all parts of the world to secure for him rare and important codices to be placed in the Medicean Library. He announced that it was his ambition to form the greatest collection of books in the world, and to throw it open to public use. Such a suggestion was almost heresy in those days! So great was his influence that the Library received its name from his.

The third Medici to play an important part in this literary history was Lorenzo's son, Cardinal Giovanni, afterwards Pope Leo X. The library itself had been confiscated by the Republic during the troublous times in which Charles VIII of France played his part, and sold to the monks of San Marco; but when better times returned Cardinal Giovanni bought it back into the family, and established it in the Villa Medici in Rome. During the fourteen years the collection remained in his possession, Giovanni, as Pope Leo X, enriched it by valuable additions. On his death, in 1521, his executor, a cousin, Giulio de' Medici, afterwards Pope Clement VII, commissioned Michelangelo to erect a building worthy of housing, so precious a collection; and in 1522 the volumes were returned to Florence.

Lorenzo's promise to throw the doors open to the public was accomplished on June 11, 1571. At that time there were 3,000 precious manuscripts, most of which are still available to those who visit Florence. A few are missing.

The princes who followed Cosimo II were not so conscious of their responsibilities, and left the care of the Library to the Chapter of the Church of San Lorenzo. During this period the famous manuscript copy of Cicero's work, the oldest in existence, disappeared. Priceless miniatures were cut from some of the volumes, and single leaves from others. Where did they go? The *Cicero* has never since been heard of, but the purloining of fragments of Laurenziana books undoubtedly completed imperfections in similar volumes in other collections.

The House of Lorraine, which succeeded the House of Medici, guarded the Laurenziana carefully, placing at its head the learned Biscioni.

After him came Bandini, another capable librarian, under whose administration various smaller yet valuable collections were added in their entirety. Del Furia continued the good work, and left behind a splendid catalogue of the treasures entrusted to him. These four volumes are still to be found in the Library. In 1808, and again in 1867, the libraries of the suppressed monastic orders were divided between the Laurentian and the Magliabecchian institutions; and in 1885, through the efforts of Pasquale Villari, the biographer of Machiavelli, the Ashburnham collection, numbering 1887 volumes, was added through purchase by the Italian Government.

"Now," said Biagi, as he finished the story, "I am ready to show you some of the Medici treasures. I call them my children. They have always seemed that to me. My earliest memory is of peeping out from the back windows of the Palazzo dei della Vacca, where I was born, behind the bells of San Lorenzo, at the campanile of the ancient church, and at the Chapel of the Medici. The Medici coat of arms was as familiar to me as my father's face, and the 'pills' that perpetuated Old Cosimo's fame as a chemist possessed so great a fascination that I never rested until I became the Medicean librarian."

THE SPELL OF THE LAURENZIANA

Biagi led the way from his private office through the Hall of Tapestries. As we passed by the cases containing such wealth of illumination, only partially concealed by the green curtains drawn across the glass, I instinctively paused, but my guide insisted.

"We will return here, but first you must see the Tribuna."

We passed through the great hall into a high-vaulted, circular reading-room.

"This was an addition to the Library in 1841," Biagi explained, "to house the 1200 copies of original editions from the fifteenth-century Presses, presented by the Count Angiolo Maria d'Elchi. Yes—" he added, reading my thoughts as I glanced around; "this room is a distinct blemish. The great Buonarroti must have turned in his grave when it was finished. But the volumes themselves will make you forget the architectural blunder."

He showed me volumes printed from engraved blocks by the Germans, Sweynheym and Pannartz, at Subiaco, in the first Press established in Italy. I held in my hand Cicero's *Epistolæ ad Familiares*, a volume printed in 1469. In the *explicit* the printer, not at all ashamed of his accomplishment, adds in Latin:

285

IN QUEST OF THE PERFECT BOOK

John, from within the town of Spires, was the first to print books in Venice from bronze types. See, O Reader, how much hope there is of future works when this, the first, has surpassed the art of penmanship

There was Tortelli's *Orthographia dictionum e Græcia tractarum*, printed in Venice by Nicolas Jenson, showing the first use of Greek characters in a printed book. The Aldine volumes introduced me to the first appearance of Italic type. No wonder that Italy laid so firm a hand upon the scepter of the new art, when Naples, Milan, Ferrara, Florence, Piedmont, Cremona, and Turin vied with Venice in producing such examples!

"You must come back and study them at your leisure," the librarian suggested, noting my reluctance to relinquish the volume I was inspecting to receive from him some other example equally interesting. "Now I will introduce you to the prisoners, who have never once complained of their bondage during all these centuries."

In the great hall we moved in and out among the *plutei*, where Biagi indicated first one manuscript and then another, with a few words of explanation as to the significance of each.

"No matter what the personal bent of any man," my guide continued, "we have here in the Library that which will satisfy his intellectual

286

desires. If he is a student of the Scriptures, he will find inspiration from our sixth-century *Syriac Gospels*, or the *Biblia Amiatina*. For the lawyer, we have the *Pandects of Justinian*, also of the sixth century, which even today form the absolute basis of Roman law. What classical scholar could fail to be thrilled by the fourth-century *Medicean Virgil*, with its romantic history, which I will tell you some day; what lover of literature would not consider himself privileged to examine Boc-caccio's manuscript copy of the *Decameron*, or the Petrarch manuscript on vellum, in which appear the famous portraits of Laura and Petrarch; or Benvenuto Cellini's own handwriting in his autobiography? We must talk about all these, but it would be too much for one day."

Leading the way back to his sanctum, Biagi left me for a moment. He returned with some manuscript poems, which he turned over to me.

"This shall be the climax of your first day in the Laurenziana," he exclaimed. "You are now holding Michelangelo in your lap!"

Can you wonder that the week I had allotted to Florence began to seem too brief a space of time? In response to the librarian's suggestion I returned to the Library day after day. He was profligate in the time he gave me. Together we studied the *Biblia Amiatina,* the very copy brought from England to Rome in 716 by Ceolfrid, Abbot of Wearmouth, intended as a votive offering at the Holy Sepulchre of Saint Peter. By this identification at the Laurenziana in 1887 the volume became one of the most famous in the world. In the plate opposite the Prophet Ezra is shown by the artist sitting before a book press filled with volumes bound in crimson covers of present-day fashion, and even the book in which Ezra is writing has a binding. It was a new thought to me that the binding of books such as we know it was in practice as early as the eighth century.

At another time we examined the *Medicean Virgil* written on vellum, dating back to the fourth century, and the oldest Codex of the Latin poet.

"This is a veritable treasure for the classical scholar, is it not?" Biagi inquired. "While the Medicean collection remained in the hands of the Chapter of San Lorenzo some vandal cut out the first leaves. See,—the text now begins at the 48th line of the 6th Eclogue."

I felt almost as if I were looking at a mutilated body, so precious did the manuscript seem.

"In 1799," the librarian continued, "these sheets were carried to France as part of the Napoleonic booty. Later, through the good

288

THE PROPHET EZRA. From *Codex Amiatinus*, (6th Century)
Showing earliest Volumes in Bindings
Laurenziana Library, Florence (12 x 8)

offices of Prince Metternich, under a special article in the Treaty of Vienna, the volume was returned to Italy. In 1816 a solemn festival was held here in Florence to celebrate its restoration to the Library. Such events as these," Biagi added, "show you the place the book holds in the hearts of the Italian people. Look!" he exclaimed, pointing disgustedly at the stiff, ugly binding placed upon the *Virgil* in Paris during its captivity. "See how little the French appreciated what this volume really is!"

The Petrarch manuscript yielded me the originals of the famous portraits of Madonna Laura de Noves de Sale and of Messer Francesco Petrarca which had hung in my library for years; my friend's comments made them assume a new meaning. The poet's likeness so closely resembles other more authentic portraits that we may accept that of Madonna Laura as equally correct, even though the same opportunity for comparison is lacking. What could be more graceful or original than the dressing of the hair, recalling the elegance of the *coiffures* worn by the ladies of Provence and France rather than of Italy, even as the little pearl-sewn cap is absolutely unknown in the fashions of Petrarch's native country. After looking at the painting, we can understand the inspiration for Petrarch's lines:

IN QUEST OF THE PERFECT BOOK

Say from what vein did Love procure the gold
To make those sunny tresses? From what thorn
Stole he the rose, and whence the dew of morn,
Bidding them breathe and live in Beauty's mould?

So we discussed the treasures which were laid out before me as I returned again and again to the Library. The illuminated volumes showed me that marvelous Book of Hours Francesco d'Antonio made for Lorenzo the Magnificent, which is described in an earlier chapter (*page* 146); I became familiar with the gorgeous pages of Lorenzo Monaco, master of Fra Angelico; of Benozzo Gozzoli, whose frescoes give the Riccardi its greatest fame; of Gherado and Clovio, and other great artists whose names are unknown or forgotten.

Besides being librarian of the Laurenziana, Biagi was also custodian of the Buonarroti and the da Vinci archives. Thus it was that during some of my visits I had the opportunity to study the early sketches of the great Leonardo, and the manuscript letters of Michelangelo. Such intimacies gave me an understanding of the people and the times in which they worked that has clothed that period with an everlasting halo.

As our friendship expanded through our work

together, Biagi introduced me to other fascinations, outside the Library. I came to know Pasquale Villari and other great Italian intellects. My friend and I planned Odysseys together,—to Vallom-brosa, to Pisa, to Perugia, to Siena. We visited the haunts of Dante.

Nor was our conversation devoted wholly to the literary spirits of antiquity. One day some-thing was said about George Eliot. I had always shared the common fallacy that she was entitled to be classified as the greatest realist of the analytical or psychological school; yet I had always marveled at the consummate skill which made it possible for her, in *Romola,* to draw her characters and to secure the atmosphere of veritable Italians and the truest Italy without herself having lived amongst the Florentines and assimilating those unique peculiarities which she so wonderfully portrayed. For I had accepted the myth that she had only passed through Italy on her memorable trip with the Brays in 1849, and secured her local color by study.

I made some allusion to this, and Biagi smiled.

"Where did you get that idea?" he asked. "Her diary tells you to the contrary."

I could only confess that I had never read her diary.

"George Eliot and Lewes were in Florence together in 1861," he continued; "and it was because they were here that *Romola* became a fact."

Enjoying my surprise, the librarian became more communicative:

"They studied here together from May 4 until June 7, 1861, at the Magliabecchian Library," said he, "and I can tell you even the titles of the books they consulted."

Perhaps I showed my incredulity.

"I have discovered the very slips which Lewes signed when he took out the volumes," he continued. "Would you like to see them?"

By this time Biagi knew me too well to await my response. So we walked together over to the Biblioteca Nazionale Centrale, the library which became famous two hundred and fifty years ago through the reputation of a jeweler's shop boy, Antonio Magliabecchi, and was known as the Biblioteca Magliabecchiana for more than a century before the Biblioteca Palatina was joined with it in 1860 under its present modern and unromantic name.

As we walked along Biagi told me of the unique personality of this Magliabecchi, which attracted the attention of the literary world while he was

ANTONIO MAGLIABECCHI
Founder of the Magliabecchia Library, Florence

collecting the nucleus of the library. Dibdin scouted him, declaring that his existence was confined to the "parade and pacing of a library," yet so great was his knowledge and so prodigious his memory that when the Grand Duke of Florence asked him one day for a particular volume, he was able to reply:

"The only copy of this work is at Constantinople, in the Sultan's library, the seventeenth volume in the second bookcase on the right as you go in."

We entered the old reading hall, which is almost the only portion of the building still remaining as it was when George Eliot and George Henry Lewes pursued their studies at one of the massive walnut tables. The jeering bust of Magliabecchi is still there; the same volumes, resting upon their ornamental shelves, still await the arrival of another genius to produce another masterpiece—but except for these the Library has become as modernized as its name.

"I was going over some dusty receipts here one day," my friend explained, "which I found on the top of a cupboard in the office of the archives. It was pure curiosity. I was interested in the names of many Italian writers who have since become famous, but when I stumbled upon a number of receipts signed 'G. H. Lewes,' I realized that I was on the track of some valuable material. These I arranged chronologically, and this is what I found."

Now let me go back a little, before, with Biagi's help, I fit these interesting receipts into the story of the writing of the book as told by George Eliot's diary, which I immediately absorbed.

Silas Marner was finished on March 10, 1861, and on April 19 the author and Lewes "set off on our second journey to Florence." After arriving there, the diary tells us that they "have been industriously foraging in old streets and old books." Of Lewes she writes: "He was in continual distraction by having to attend to my wants, going with me to the Magliabecchian Library, and poking about everywhere on my behalf."

The first slip signed by Lewes is dated May 15, 1861, and called for Ferrario's *Costume Antico e Moderno*. This book is somewhat dramatic and superficial, yet it could give the author knowledge of the historical surroundings of the characters which were growing in her mind. The following day they took out Lippi's *Malmantile*, a comic poem filled with quaint phrases and sayings which fitted well in the mouths of those characters she had just learned how to dress. Migliore's *Firenze*

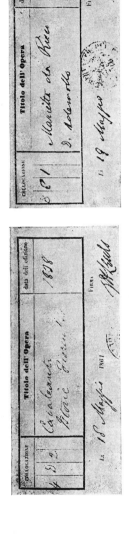

Library Slips used by George Eliot in the Magliabecchia
Library, Florence, while writing *Romola*

Illustrata and Rastrelli's *Firenze Antica e Moderna* gave the topography and the aspect of Florence at the end of the fifteenth century.

From Chiari's *Priorista* George Eliot secured the idea of the magnificent celebration of the Feast of Saint John, the effective descriptions of the cars, the races, and the extraordinary tapers. "It is the habit of my imagination," she writes in her diary, "to strive after as full a vision of the medium in which a character moves as of the character itself." Knowledge of the Bardi family, to which the author added Romola, was secured from notes on the old families of Florence written by Luigi Passerini.

"See how they came back on May 24," Biagi exclaimed, pointing to a slip calling for *Le Famiglie del Litta*, "to look in vain for the pedigree of the Bardi. But why bother," he continued with a smile; "for Romola, the Antigone of Bardo Bardi, was by this time already born in George Eliot's mind, and needed no further pedigree."

Romance may have been born, but the plot of the story was far from being clear in the author's mind. Back again in England, two months later, she writes, "This morning I conceived the plot of my novel with new distinction." On October 4,

" I am worried about my plot," and on October 7, " Began the first chapter of my novel."

Meanwhile George Eliot continued her reading, now at the British Museum. *La Vita di G. Savonarola,* by Pasquale Villari, gave her much inspiration. The book had just been published, and it may well have suggested the scene where Baldassarre Calvo meets Tito Melema on the steps of the Cathedral. No other available writer had previously described the struggle which took place for the liberation of the Lunigiana prisoners, which plays so important a part in the plot of *Romola.*

In January, 1862, George Eliot writes in her diary, " I began again my novel of *Romola.*" By February the extraordinary proem and the first two chapters were completed. " Will it ever be finished?" she asks herself. But doubt vanished as she proceeded. In May, 1863, she " killed Tito with great excitement," and June 9, " put the last stroke to *Romola*—Ebenezer !"

Since then I have re-read *Romola* with the increased interest which came from the new knowledge, and the story added to my love of Florence. Many times have I wandered, as George Eliot and Lewes did, to the heights of Fiesole, and looked down, even as they, in sunlight, and with the moon casting shadows upon the wonderful and obsessing city, wishing that my vision were strong enough to extract from it another story such as *Romola*.

Such were the experiences that extended my stay in Florence. The memory of them has been so strong and so obsessing that no year has been complete without a return to Biagi and the Laurenziana. Once, during these years, he came to America, as the Royal representative of Italy at the St. Louis Exposition (see also *page* 182). In 1916 his term as librarian expired through the limitation of age, but before he retired he completely rearranged that portion of the Library which is now open to visitors (see *page* 149). The treasures of no collection are made so easily accessible except at the British Museum.

I last visited Biagi in May, 1924. His time was well occupied by literary work, particularly on Dante, which had already given him high rank as a scholar and writer; but a distinct change had come over him. I could not fathom it until he told me that he was planning to leave Florence to take up his residence in Rome. I received the news in amazement. Then the mask fell, and he answered my unasked question.

"I can't stand it!" he exclaimed. "I can't

stay in Florence and not be a part of the Laurenziana. I have tried in vain to reconcile myself,
but the Library has been so much a fiber of my
being all my life, that something has been taken
away from me which is essential to my existence."
The spell of the Laurenziana had possessed him
with a vital grip! The following January (1925)
he died, and no physician's diagnosis will ever
contain the correct analysis of his decease
I shall always find it difficult to visualize Florence
or the Laurenziana without Guido Biagi. When
next I hold in my hands those precious
manuscripts, still chained to their ancient
plutei, it will be with even greater
reverence. They stand as sym
bols of the immutability of
learning and culture
compared with the
brief span of life
allotted to
Prince or Librarian

INDEX

INDEX

INDEX

INDEX

INDEX

INDEX

Field, Eugene, described, 38; manuscript of, 39, 41; referred to, 38, 55

Fielding, Henry, 163

Fiesole, the heights of, 298

Firenze Antica e Moderna, Rastrelli's, 297

Firenze Illustrata, Migliore's, 296

Fiske, Willard, 26, 27

Flemish illumination, see *Illumination, Flemish*

Fletcher, Horace, friend of Eugene Field, 41; philosophy of, 75, 82, 84; his ideas of typography, 75; page of his manuscript, 77; his dinner at Graduates Club, New Haven, 84; importance of his work, 85; his friendship with William James and Henry James, 86; letter from Henry James to, 87; visit to Lamb House, 89

Fletcherism, 75, 83

Florence, Italy, the most fascinating city in Europe, 273; early printing at, 286

Florence, the Grand Duke of, 295

Forest Lovers, the, Hewlett's, 157, 158

Foucquet, Jean, 113, 138, 140, 149

France, typographical supremacy of, 194, 215-223; loses supremacy, 223; second supremacy of, 251-258

François I, of France, becomes patron of learning and culture, 216; makes Robert Étienne "printer in Greek to the King," 216; his interest in printing, 216-221; his relations with the censors, 221; referred to, 214, 216

Frankfort, 227

Franklin, Benjamin, quoted on the Baskerville editions, 245; his letter to Baskerville, 245; at the Didot Press, 252

French illumination, see *Illumination, French*

French Republic, the, 141

French School of Painting, the, 139

Fust, John, 198, 199

Gabrilowitch, Mrs. Ossip, 172

Garamond, Claude, 220

Garnett, Dr. Richard, 164, 165; lines written by Dobson on, 166, 167, estimate of, 166

General Theological School Library, the, New York, 196

Genesis, the *Cottonian*, 117

Geneva, the Étiennes at, 223

George, Saint, 137

Germany, not sufficiently developed as nation to take advantage of Gutenberg's discovery, 8, 9; brief typographical supremacy of, 194-201; loses supremacy, 201

Gherado, 149, 290

Gilder, Richard Watson, 177

Giotto, 147, 273

Golden Gospels of Saint Médard, the, described, 127-128

Golden type, the, designed by William Morris, 18

Gold leaf, 116

Gold, Oriental, 112

Goldsmith, Oliver, 163

Gothic illumination, see *Illumination, Gothic*

Gozzoli, Benozzo, 149, 290

Graduates Club, the, in New Haven, 84

Grandjon, Robert, 228

Greece, the rich humanities of, 15

Greek classics, the, first printed by Aldus, 209

Greeks, the, 7

Greek types, 56, 219-221, 238

Grimani Breviary, the, described, 141-145, 146, 149

Grimani, Cardinal Domenico, 142, 143

Grimani, Doge Antonio, 143

Grimani, Giovanni, Patriarch of Aquileia, 142

Grimani, Marino, Patriarch of Aquileia, 142

Grolier Club of New York, the, 213

Grolier, Jean, saves the Aldine Press by his intervention, 56, 238; his friendship with family of Aldus,

307

INDEX

INDEX

310

INDEX

INDEX

Orcutt, Reginald Wilson, 165

Orcutt, William Dana, first visit to Italy, 14; meeting with Guido Biagi, 14, 277; his work designing the Humanistic type, 17–33; in the Ambrosiana Library, 24–25; experiences with Willard Fiske, 26, 27; apprenticeship at old University Press, 38; experience with Eugene Field, 38–41; experiences with Mrs. Mary Baker Eddy, 52; becomes head of University Press, 55; his ambition to emulate methods of early printers, 55; experiences with Bernard Shaw, 67–71; returns to Italy in 1903; his interest in the Bodoni and Didot types, 78; his acquaintance with Horace Fletcher, 75, 82, 84, 86; his acquaintance with Henry James, 86; visit to Lamb House, 89; experiences with William James, 90–92; experiences with Cobden-Sanderson, 96–101; experiences with Theodore Roosevelt, 101–106; becomes interested in illumination, 111; meeting with Maurice Hewlett, 155–162; experiences with Austin Dobson, 162–169; experiences with Mark Twain, 170–177; experiences with Charles Eliot Norton, 178–183; experiences with William Dean Howells, 183–188; experiences in the Laurenziana Library, 273–300; last visit with Guido Biagi, 299–300

Orcutt, Mrs. William Dana, 165, 171

Oriental gold, 112

Orthographia dictionum e Graecia tractarum, Tortelli's, 286

Oxford, Edward Harley, 2d Earl of, 136

PALATINA, the Biblioteca, at Florence, 293

Pan and the Young Shepherd, Hewlett's, 159

Paper, poorer quality introduced, 238; Italian handmade, 238; French handmade, 238, 257; Baskerville the first to introduce glossy, 250

Parchment, English, 29; Florentine, 28; Roman, 28; virgin, 113

Paris, 227

Paris Exposition of 1801, the, 258

Passerini, Luigi, 297

Patmore, Coventry, 89

Patrons, Italian, attitude toward printed book of, 11; their conception of a book, 11; their real reasons for opposing the art of printing, 12, 151

Peignot foundry, the, in Paris, 80

Persia, 118

Perugia, 291

Petrarca, Francesco, the father of humanism, 15; Italic type said to be based upon handwriting of, 17, 210; portrait of, 287, 289; quoted, 290

Petrarch, see *Petrarca, Francesco*

Petrarch, the *Humanistic*, the type design, 17–26; the copy, 26, 27; the illustrations, 28; the parchment, 28; the ink, 29, 30; the composition, 30; Norton's estimate of, 32

Philip, of Burgundy, 135

Philip II, of Spain, 227; his interest in Plantin's *Biblia Polyglotta*, 227–228, 233; makes Plantin *phototypographe*, 233

Pickering, the London publisher, revives the old-style type, 251

Piedmont, early printing at, 286

Pierpont Morgan Library, the, New York, 99, 196

Pisa, 291

Pius XI, Pope, see *Ratti, Achille*

Plantin, Christophe, financially embarrassed by his *Biblia Polyglotta*, 56, 238; his Greek types, 221; leaves France, 223; conception and making of his *Biblia Polyglotta*, 227–233; his types, 228; his printer's mark, 228, 236; made *phototypographe* by Philip II, 233; the value

INDEX

INDEX

INDEX

315

INDEX

THIS VOLUME is composed in Poliphilus type, reproduced by the Lanston Monotype Corporation, London, from the Roman face designed in 1499 by Francesco Griffo, of Bologna, for Aldus Manutius, and originally used in the *Hypnerotomachia Poliphili*. The Italic is based upon that designed for Antonio Blado, Printer to the Holy See from 1515 to 1567.

The cover, a modern adaptation of the Grolier design used on Capella: *L'Anthropologia*, is designed by Enrico Monetti.

The illustrations, many now appearing in book form for the first time, were secured chiefly through the courtesy of the librarians of the British Museum, London; the Bibliothèque Nationale, Paris; the Laurenziana Library, Florence; the Ambrosiana Library, Milan; the Marciana Library, Venice; the Vatican Library, Rome; and from private collectors.

The plates of the illustrations were made by the Walker Engraving Company, New York City, and are printed on DeJonge's Art Mat. The text paper is Warren's Olde Style.

The typography, presswork, and binding are by the Plimpton Press, Norwood, Massachusetts, under the personal supervision of William Dana Orcutt.